WEAPON: MOUTH

WEAPON: MOUTH

Adventures in the Free Speech Zone

STONEY BURKE

WITH A
FOREWORD
by **Paul Krassner**

Regent Press
Berkeley, California

Table of Contents

FOREWORD

by

Paul Krassner

Stoney Burke and I have a couple of things in common. Some people think I'm Paul Kantner, and some people think Stoney is Wavy Gravy. Also, Stoney and I are both political satirists, but he's more courageous than I am. Whereas I perform on a stage for a paying audience, he stands on a box outdoors at college campuses for students who were just passing by, but like a human magnet his passionate ranting serves to morph them into a crowd. I use a microphone; he doesn't. Nobody would ever think that he had once been a mime.

Lenny Bruce was arrested many times, ostensibly for his language, though actually for his taboo-breaking irreverence toward religious and political targets. Now stand-up comics would never dream of being imprisoned for what they had said. Except Stoney. He's been busted twenty times.

Usually, what's left of his hair is dyed green and he wears baggy clown pants, but in 1984 he wore an Uncle Sam costume at the Democratic convention in San Francisco to cover the event for KPFA. He got inside Moscone Center on the basis of a security pass that somebody left in a telephone booth. Stoney crawled over a velvet rope, but five minutes into his oration about homelessness, he was in handcuffs once again. This time, by the grace of a quartet of Secret Service agents, he ended up in a psych ward, where he was held for eight hours before being released.

"The doctor went to bat for me," Stoney explains, "once I told him I didn't wear those clothes all the time."

This book *Weapon: Mouth* serves as a nice slice of free speech in the pizza of countercultural history. Its title is excerpted from a Berkeley police blotter. Under the heading, "Describe weapon, instrument, equipment, trick, device, or force used," here's the response: "Mouth, voice." By any other name, it would still be a treat to read. Enjoy your ass off.

— PAUL KRASSNER

Paul Krassner is the author of
WHO'S TO SAY WHAT'S OBSCENE:
POLITICS, CULTURE, AND COMEDY IN AMERICA TODAY

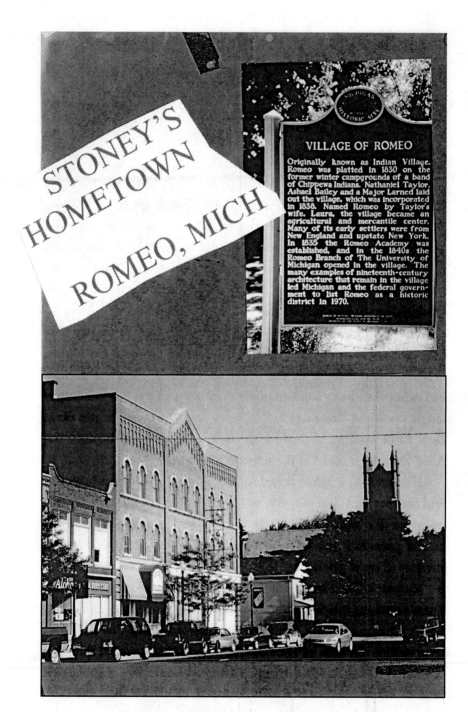

STONEY'S HOMETOWN ROMEO, MICH

VILLAGE OF ROMEO

Originally known as Indian Village, Romeo was platted in 1830 on the former winter campgrounds of a band of Chippewa Indians. Nathaniel Taylor, Ashael Bailey and a Major Larned laid out the village, which was incorporated in 1838. Named Romeo by Taylor's wife, Laura, the village became an agricultural and mercantile center. Many of its early settlers were from New England and upstate New York. In 1835 the Romeo Academy was established, and in the 1840s the Romeo Branch of The University of Michigan opened in the village. The many examples of nineteenth-century architecture that remain in the village led Michigan and the federal government to list Romeo as a historic district in 1970.

Stoney's Home Town

Stoney's Hometown

Just off the highway in northern Macomb County, where the flat-smooth drabness of the suburbs finally gives way to long stretches of greenery, is my hometown. With its scattered orchards and touristy roadside stands, Romeo Michigan is the gateway to the vast landmass known as "Up North." But it's not quite "Up" or "North." For me, it was a central place to begin hitchhiking all over the 48 states. And it was home.

The stifling need to flee would always give way to homey feelings for Romeo upon my return. I had slept for far too many nights, in abandoned cars, or in the wilderness area of the local park to feel otherwise. Betty Burke's home cooking and Jim Burke's hearty laugh would be like music to my ears once I walked in the door, back from another venture into the great unknown beyond the A&W Root Beer stand at the edge of town.

Hitchhiking is space travel for poor people. Before adulthood and fear set in, I had covered all 48 states. But, as they say, there's no place like home. Home was where I had strategically flunked out of parochial school, and found my spirit in the woods and streams of rural Michigan.

Romeo is like a lot of small towns and villages – on the surface, there's nothing much going on, but lift the lid and bang on the pot, and it's a not-so-subtle cauldron of various activity. For instance, long before the start of the Civil War, the Underground Railroad carried runaway slaves through Romeo, and on to Canada. This part of my hometown's history had not been well documented, but thanks to the Romeo Historical Society, secret pages and clues from the past unfold, revealing the abolitionist's trail. All of this a long time before the Burke family decided to set down roots. These were the golden days of small-town America. At one time in Romeo, a village of say 2500, we had no less than 13 gas stations, a movie theater, and an A&W root beer stand. I remember walking down past the Romeo Theater one day in the late 1950's, and the poster of THE BLOB jumped out at me. The Outer Limits warned me not to adjust the TV set. There was something strange going on in the land. Elvis was just coming out of hiding from bad cinema. The draft for the Vietnam war was looming, and the assassin's bullet was striking everywhere.

The Romeo Theater closed in 1968, and some local hippies turned the place into music venue called THE MOTHERS. On one occasion, Romeo's own band, the Air Speed Indica*tor,* would open for the MC5. Then one night Iggy and The Stooge*s* brought their thunder-grind surge of power chords to Romeo. Shortly into their set, Iggy Pop decided to take his pants off and run through the crowd. Iggy has been known to do that, but this was northern Macomb County. Cops are called. THE MOTHERS is closed. It was too late. I had seen the crazed look on Iggy's face as his band pounded a haze of meat-grinding feedback. He assaulted and clawed at anything that moved. THAT was rock 'n' roll.

One-Eyed Mailbox

The cold spring air could not reach me under the thick covers as my transistor radio's earpiece scratched static with every of gust of the wind outside. The Beatles are all in harmony as they sing, "She loves you yeah yeah yeah yeah." I am around 10 years old. I roll over, burrow in, and adjust the tuner to bring CKLW in loud and clear. It's a Saturday morning sometime in the early 1960's in Romeo, Michigan. Just as "three big hits in a row" blasts in my earpiece, my father walks briskly into my bedroom with a bucket of suds, a wire brush, and a serious look on his face. Dad was old school about chores, and one did not feign to "forget" or slack off from doing them. To my father, an industrial arts teacher, hard work was a virtue. Monday through Friday we had our routine. It was up early for school, back home for dinner at 6 pm, do the dishes, feed the dog, homework, maybe one TV show a night. Then off to bed. That's where the transistor radio, with the handy earpiece, comes in. Under the covers, in the dark, the music never stops, and the call of the wild world could be tuned in, if you held very still. And if the big tree outside your window was not being buffeted by the wind.

This particular morning was quite tense indeed with Dad bursting into the room and jostling me awake. He grumbled for me to hurry along. I was really hoping this was not some new chore routine to add to my already busy Saturday. My father's temperament was honed in the depression era. As a WWII vet it was rise and shine no need to sit on your pity potty, procrastination was just so much stale oatmeal. I scrambled out of bed and quickly dressed.

I was half right. It was work all right, more like a "something has happened in the middle of the night" kind of chore, and NOW is the time to clean it up.

As a kid, I was vaguely aware at the time of my parent's involvement with Project HOPE. This church-based group brought together people of many faiths to attempt to address decades of intolerance and Jim Crow aftertaste. Were these gatherings being watched? Perhaps it was my parents' renting of the upstairs apartment to a young African-American woman that pushed the local bigots over the edge. We will never know. Whatever it was, it brought out the worst in somebody.

When I finally dragged myself out of bed and got my clothes on, my father was already out in front on Bailey Street. He was looking down on the sidewalk as if some maggot-infested road kill had crawled its way there and died again. As I got closer and joined him, I could see him staring at big thick letters written in black tar. The letters spelled out "NIGR LUVRS." The letters were large enough to take up the entire width of the sidewalk in front of our house. Just above the racial slur was an arrow pointing to our front door. This ignorant bozo wanted to make sure exactly what home had violated his lily-white code of conduct.

My father handed me the soap bucket and brush. I set about scrubbing it off. The hours seemed to drag by. The thick tar letters, like racism itself, were not easy to make disappear. I was still working on the "G" when the noontime church bells rang downtown. In the past, I had heard my mother Betty describe how the local hamburger joint refused to serve people of color, or worse, served frozen meat patties "to go" to the unsuspecting with an evil smirk. That was until Betty Burke and some friends decided to have lunch there with "whomever" they chose, as many times as they wanted, and shamed the owners into changing their menu.

I kept scrubbing the tar slurs until my knees hurt.

By now word had spread quickly in our small town about what

had happened the night before. People who you thought were your friends just shrugged it off and yawned, while folks who you'd never guess had a tolerant bone in their bodies would grab a brush and help me clean it off.

It wasn't too long before a knucklehead in a brown pick-up had circled the block maybe a half dozen times, honking his horn, spinning his wheels, and leering like a malt-shop zombie. I took a break from scrubbing and stood up to get a good look at him. I was to be reminded of that face for the next ten years, as he was a longtime village resident who lived a few blocks down from us on another street.

He would call my name at sporting events or slow down his truck to say, "Hi Stoney." He knew that I knew what we all knew. Life in a small town is not all it's cracked up to be and a far cry from *Mayberry RFD*.

I finally have the letters washed off the sidewalk. My father motions for me to join him as he closely examines the mailbox. Sure enough, this same person, or an accomplice, had shot a hole in our mailbox; a bullet had left a hole the size of a dime. A mere six inches higher, and a hot chunk of lead would have entered our living room where the Project HOPE meeting was taking place. Thankfully, this half wit could not spell or shoot straight.

Many seasons have passed since then. It's been over 50 years now and almost all vestiges of that night have vanished, except for one thing. Jim Burke never replaced that one-eyed, bullet-scarred mailbox. That mailbox has been a reminder to me my whole life that standing up for your convictions can be dangerous. To do nothing and turn your head only encourages evil and delays the solution.

Last year Jim took a picture of his "Obama for President" sign next to the wounded mailbox. It's an image I'll let speak for itself. But the irony is not lost on me, nor will it ever be.

You could still see my father on occasion, over those many

years, run his thick, calloused finger over the bullet hole. My father, Jim Burke, never gave up his quest for social justice and went on to be a founding member of CROP Walk, as well as many other local causes, in the decades that followed.

Jim Burke passed on December 12, 2009. As the undertaker and his son were working their way down the front steps with his corpse, the gurney seemed to pause, and for just a moment I was sure I could see my father shift his head slightly and open one eye, just to see if that mailbox was still there. Damn right it was!

The next week an official from the Romeo Historical Society came by to get the mailbox. It sits today on display with much older exhibits from the Underground Railroad. For one stop along that journey, Jim Burke was the conductor, with a safe haven.

Granted, the USA might be just a few stamps short of freedom, but it's people like Jim Burke who have made Romeo, Michigan, a place where small-town history is stamped, delivered, and remembered.

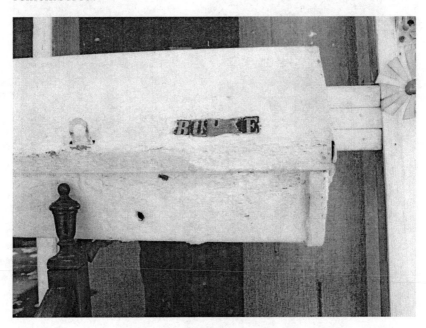

One-Eyed Mailbox

Photo: Lauren Hatvany

Stoney In The Sand

Stoney Burke

I was born in Highland Park, Michigan, and I lived in an orphanage for two years. When I was two and a half years old, my parents, who were my foster parents, adopted me from Highland Park and brought me to a place thirty miles north of Detroit. Then they took me up to a place called Romeo, Michigan, and there I grew up for twenty-three years.

My parents were, back in the sixties, by no means radical, but they taught me the "all people should be treated equal" sort of thing, and they got involved in the civil rights movement. I remember as a child they would always tell us about all the racism that went on in this little town of ours, so we always kind of knew who the good guys and the bad guys in town were. And that was something to know! You're usually brought up taught that everybody's good.

Then, during the sixties, not me, but my older brother and his friends started getting radicalized because of the riots that came down, and because of the anti-war movement. And I started just listening to them just as a young kid, you know. And when you're a young kid, of course, you can't really go out and march all the time because you're worrying about being a kid. You've still got your parents on top of you, and you've still got junior high on top of you, and you've got your education, your future to think about. And there was one guy in particular who lived in Detroit, and he used to talk to us about really heavy stuff – the Weathermen, and what sexism is, and racism, and "this is the worker's attitude."

So I started getting a hold on it real young. But I'd never found a way to express it until I got frustrated enough to really do it, and start to explore it like I do now on college campuses. I never really had the venue for it. You can't make money. I mean, I ain't got no money. Hollywood's not going to hire me talking about the things I do. Oh, someday, if I let them.

But basically, because I'm here in Berkeley, I have a support system, i.e. the Avenue, Sproul Plaza and all these things. I have a support system where I can work on this and develop a political attitude about things. If I were in another place I might still be doing pantomime, and maybe opening for another performer, but that's about the best I could do.

Hitchhiking North America

There was a moment in time, or so we thought, when the eternal WAR was called off, and healing was thought to be at hand. That day and era was short lived. The meat grinder of hate turns your dreams to sawdust all over the world again. I, like many others, strapped a backpack on my back, and hitchhiked every state that had a road. Dodging the law by walking up the freeway ramp to a place called America. That Kerouac guy aroused a rambling nature in me. The big beat of rock and roll moved my soul. I could not sit still. Standing alongside a road, my thumb out for months at a time. My harmonica squeaked the blues. I put my trust in the Universe, Irish luck, and my prayers. You can learn a lot about people, and their hearts, when you have to trust them with your life.

There was the time with Roger, my hometown buddy. We hitchhiked down to Nitro, West Virginia, sleeping in rest stops, or under a billboard. Before long we had hitched down to Orlando, Florida to work construction near the new Disneyworld complex. Our company flattened orange groves to make way for subdivisions. For $3.25/hr we'd juice the land and fill in the swamps.

It did not take too long for me to find out that the south was not a place I wanted to spend the rest of my life. After being hired by a construction company, the white kid new hires were immediately put on the survey crew at .25 cents more an hour than the black laborers who had been there for over 20 years. It did not take more than a second invite to a KKK meeting, that I decided to put my thumb back out, and head to a different mindset. I learned more about the USA and the back roads of free speech in those days of hitchhiking than I could ever put in words. The world is a bigger and more complicated place than I had ever imagined. In all my travels, it was the great West that caught my eye and soul. A lot of history in this country moves from West to East. I wanted to be a part of that.

At First I Said Nothing

College towns used to run wild with jugglers, Bible thumpers, and folk-singing heroes. Where have they all gone? The robots and fake social networks have a cybercafé of blinking cursor lights to showcase the "spontaneous" events that shape our lives.

I believe in our true nature. I believe that the depth of our belief in life comes in unrefined and unscripted moments – a lightning flash of thought that lets us know that if we lost electricity, and if all of the TVs, computers, and smartphones went down, we would survive as a species. Our mind's garden would bloom and swoon until the lights came back on.

The hard-wired iPodians and button-rubbing Googleites now infest the minds of once-curious students, but there was a time when a creative or eccentric busker could find a Spot and work it into a life. (Ahem.) Like ME! Those days are sadly disappearing. What was once private is now public. One thing we can all agree on however is that no one is ever going to get rich, form an army, and take over a small country with the money earned from busking.

Imagine a performance with no electric lights, no volume-controlled sounds, floating 3D web page, or wireless brain. A world where the only social networking site is the one made of actual human people you gather into a circle. The world of StoneySpeaks!

Long long ago in the early 70s, I was smitten by the simple, yet powerful, medium of MIME. After taking several classes at the University of Oregon, completing a long residence with famed movement teacher Leonard Pitt, and much research, I became

one of those pesky mimes. Not a bad one, either. I look back at my
white face, black tights, and handwritten title cards and I cringe
– in a good way. The concept of telling a story or getting a laugh
without making a sound is still a Luddite song worth singing.

My highlight gig as a mime was the night I opened up for the
Firesign Theatre at the University of Oregon in the late '70s. The
place was packed, I was opening for legends, and the crowd was
more than generous with its applause.

The mellow life in Eugene was fine for a few years, but something began to smell, and I was losing my edge. I headed straight
for the San Francisco Bay Area. At the Leonard Pitt School of
Mime, I spent two and a half years, five days a week, learning to
move every twitch in my hitch. The training was so good I ended
up peeling off my white face forever.

When you perform on the streets, you are automatically put
in a unique class of performer – not better, just different. A street
performer's motives for flinging himself directly into the grinding
wheel of public scrutiny can be as varied as the weather. Over the
years, a few have made a lasting impression on me, and I can name
more than a few I've wondered about from afar. Perhaps you know
of a few in your particular corner of the world?

Almost everyone can remember a TV show, or a movie, that
influenced their lives in some way. The street performer's life is
not that story. Rather, it's a glance at the sideshow of real life – a
look at people who may never see the green side of show business,
or at those whose dreams are beyond the seas on which they sail.
What can I say? My kind of people!

Before there were governments and organized religions,
there were minstrels and storytellers who traveled from village
to village and spread the songs, jokes, and news of the day. They
were valued by those who *knew,* and reviled by those whose taste in
entertainment ran more to the pleasing of monarchs and priests.
Like these, their predecessors, the minstrels of today are, even

now through Google and YouTube, putting on their performing faces and walking down to the Plaza. The world waits there with coins, or just free coffee.

Stoney in Tights

Silent man speaks By Jim Paulin

"I get scared, but its different, because there's a white face between me and the audience . . . but the fear makes me better . . . the only difference between now and grades one through 12 is a white face . . . I was always sort of crazy . . . mother; "Yes, my son was always crazy," said mime Pat Burke, discussing stage fright, and briefly departing from his visual medium to orally mimic his mother.

Burke, 24, originally from Romeo, Michigan, a Detroit suburb, now lives in and is in love with Eugene, Oregon. The tools of his trade are also his transportation vehicle, i.e., he hitch-hiked from Oregon to Amherst, via the Mariposa Folk Festival, in Toronto, where he did a skit with David Bromberg providing the background music.

Hitching at the toll booths on I-90 in Albany, N.Y., he was trying to get a ride by doing mime for the passing cars, and was arrested for hitchhiking. He was fined $5.00 after being told "get into the car, smartass" by a New York State policeman who wasn't amused. In Hartford, he had the stage for 15 minutes at "Good Old Times," a bar. He passed the hat afterwards and earned $13; he was also offered a full-time job as an entertainer.

Previous experience includes working at a playground, which he still enjoys doing, but now as a mime: "Kids are the best audience, so aware, and they laugh and laugh and laugh. He said that whenever he calls a day care center or school to offer to put on a show, the administrators are overjoyed.

More recently, he belonged to a clown club, and even made a guest appearance at the Shrine circus when it was in Eugene. However, he became disillusioned with clowning, due to its "sexist, racist, classist status," e.g., he considers Emmet Kelley's bum act classist. Also, he said that a clown has less flexibility than a mime, as a clown "tells his story with his clothes." Moreover, he said a clown act involves black comedy (e.g. – The Three Stooges – by hitting people or falling down).

When asked if he was a professional, he said, "Sometimes, when I pass the hat." He took one mime course in college, and has spent the rest of his pantomime education learning by doing, "learning illusions."

His present goal is to eventually go to San Francisco and join the San Francisco Mime Troupe. But currently, he is, as he put it, "a traveling minstrel," laying over in Amherst at a friend's house, and is en route to Ontario, after he hits the Boston Common and Harvard Square. In spite of a faster-paced lifestyle than Oregon, he likes Massachusetts even though "it's not quite on the ball like Oregon."

Eugene, Oregon, the Rain, Kesey, and Animal House

When I rolled into Eugene in the late '70s, the place was awash with one might call hippie heaven culture. There was a funny smell coming from the pulp mill, but just beyond that, by golly, real mountains. Everything you thought about the '60s seemed to be alive and well in Oregon. Collectives, communes, farmers markets, the WOW hall music scene, and cheap rent. If I thought I had missed the '60s, it was back to the future for me.

I lived in a place we dubbed the Anthill. Aptly named in that it was a three-bedroom house divided into a home where an odd collection of 15 people lived. My rent was $35.00 a month. All this a mere three blocks from campus. Back then, being on food stamps, and being enrolled at the University was about as good as it gets, when you have no money.

One day I was walking by a group of run-down frat houses, and a film crew was making the house look even worse than it was. This was to be known as the "Animal House." Since I was enrolled at the University of Oregon at the time, I saw a lot of the stars and crew around the campus. John Belushi was getting his haircut in the lobby of the student union one day. I stopped to talk to him as he sat motionless in the barber chair getting his hair plumed for a big scene in the cafeteria. I had nothing else better to do that day, and ended up being an unpaid extra in the food fight scene in the 1978 film *Animal House.*

In the summers I worked for the US Forest Service, living in the rustic barracks of Blue River, Oregon. Countless hours of backbreaking work cutting fire trails and witnessing criminal clear cuts. I had never seen a tornado made of fire before. One stood over me and paused, the embers smoking up my plaid shirt as I back up impotently with my fire hose. This was not a job I could do any more.

Ken Kesey, noted author and prankster, lived nearby in Springfield, Oregon. One day in 1976, he announced that he was going to audition everyone and anyone for an event called the HOO HAW. After nearly a week of every kind of act you could think of trying out on the open stage, Kesey announced that everyone had passed the audition. He rented out MacArthur Court at the University. Then he brought in the likes of satirist Paul Krassner, jazz musician Charles Lloyd, writer William Burroughs. The list goes on. Another space and time where I can say ... I was there!

The Open Ward, Jonestown, Harvey Milk, and the Frog House

I was pumping gas for a living when I first got to Berkeley, California. I was working the pumps the night Harvey Milk was assassinated by the Twinkie-defense killer Dan White. Ten days later Jim Jones and Peoples Temple massacre splashed itself all over the SF Bay Area landscape. California can be a place of crazies and contradictions coming head to head.

A woman leans out of her car and asks if I heard the news? Harvey Milk has been shot. Ten days later I'm filling up a truck and the guy asks the same question. The Peoples Temple massacre. This all in my first month of California living. I never pumped gas again, and moved on to my next failed career: Butcher's Assistant. Yes, I know what's in hot dogs. End of story.

Where would I be if I had not crossed paths with the late great Judy Foster? Judy was a larger-than-life woman who used her skills as a cook to change the world around her, and the people she loved. Judy was the matriarch of a large house in Berkeley called the Frog House. About as close to a commune as I have ever lived in. I was living in the attic, performing on campus, and making the most of my new life in California. Every month, we'd have dinner, argue nicely, and turn the chore wheel to the next task on our list.

A big beautiful backlash against post-war techno boredom was building up. The Punks were breaking it down to three chords and slashing text, while rap was using phrasing and in-your-face critique like nothing before.

I had just finished performing at UCB one afternoon in the late '70s. There was a thunder beyond the trees in lower Sproul plaza. It was the Dead Kennedys! At first it looked like a bunch of punks had jumped the band and swallowed them as they leaped to the beat and cranked out. No, it was the grand mosh pit dance. There was a ripeness of rebellion in the air. Punk club owner Tim Yohanan would have me down to KPFA for his "Maximum RocknRoll" show. Those were the days when faking it would not get you anywhere. That was all to change when the hybrid of mass-denial Reaganism, melded with the looming ogre of 24 hr. computer consumerism.

Photo: Annie Moose

On The Berkeley Campus in the 1980's

Photo: Dave Blackman

Country Joe And Wavy Gravy

Photo: Dave Blackman

Punks, Old School Rap And Reagan

People's Park Wheelbarrow

The California sun is just warming up the lawn at People's Park in Berkeley. It's April 26, 1980. On this date in 1968, the citizens of the world took back a patch of green and scrubs from the rapacious, bulldozing fangs of the UC Regents. These Regents are the sworn enemies of the freedom-loving souls who also lay claim to this 2.5 acre patch of soil.

A small, wooden stage, a well-kept garden, and the right to hang out; three simple things, but battled over as if the future of the University depended upon it. Owned by the University, patrolled by their police, but lived upon by people kicked butt-backwards into the abyss of the have-nots. One could almost think that the entire freshman class had never even seen a homeless person before. Well, I guess if Walt Disney never had the homeless in the Magic Kingdom, why should Berkeley?

Many words, documents, and first-hand accounts can take you back to that day in 1968. From the occupation of People's Park, to the murder of James Rector, to the still ongoing battle over a chunk of open land in the middle of Berkeley. The following is not that history of People's Park. I encourage you to seek that out. Rather, this is the short history of one afternoon and two chaotic nights, of the volcanic struggle over the use of the People's Park stage, over who would control the volume, the people or the state.

This is not an uncommon story, I'm sure, but People's Park is an uncommon place. Even more uncommon in the year 1980, when head rancher Ronald Reagan finally made it to central command of the beef and bull. When Reagan was the Governor of

California, he swore to, "Get those Commies at People's Park." He hadn't mellowed in the twelve years since making that comment. No process had been established, in the interim, to grant a sound permit, or the right to organize, in the Park. No mechanism to ensure that our constitutional rights to Free Speech and peaceful assembly would be recognized.

On this given Sunday, the anniversary of the original occupation, there was not a soul up and down the avenue who did not know that there was to be a concert with bands and special guests. Bear in mind that this was BC (Before Computers), and word travelled by mouth or Xeroxed leaflet. The various, colorful representatives from Punk-land and Hippie-village gathered hours before the noon starting time. On this, the day of rest, the smoking of the best, chased with a beer or two, began with the dawn. Our recreation continued right up until it was time to plug the cord into the socket. The UCPD (University of California Police Department) began its walk-throughs and its perimeter hassles at about the time the first sound-check rattled the neighbors' windows. We thought we had a valid sound permit, an agreement to agree, that at least until the fog rolled in at sunset, we'd have the right to stretch out on the lawn and choke on the dust swirled up by the dancers. When the mushroom heads started whirling and the bubble-lady sent her little soapy orbs throbbing to the Funky Nixons, we got a dose of the B-Town Cosmic Dream.

Even with all of this love power in the air, there was an underlying tension in the atmosphere. Behind us, in a small parking lot, two police vans disgorged a platoon of riot cops. No way could they dance with all of those death tools hanging from their belts. We came to party; they came to fight. We had it wrong when we thought that peace was to be the mood of the day. The clock on the Campanile chimes high noon. The first band starts picking up that big beat, the guitar screeches, the dancers twirl, and old friends meet. Suddenly, two police officers and a Suit-Wearing-Tie

Photo: Dave Blackman

Takeover Telegraph June 1980

moved very close to the lone (and highly guarded) electrical outlet. Salty, the head gardener, and the park organizers were in a heated exchange with the police ... so very close to the plug. The band, like all bands trained to play until the power is cut, continued to play. The Darth Vader-suited riot cops were now just across the street.

Faster than you could say "what the hek," the music stopped, with only the snap of the snare drum to torture the dancers with the remembrance of what they would not taste that day. For one pregnant moment, the day moves in slow motion. There is a collective feeling of outrage. Did they just pull the plug on our party?

Suddenly, from the back of the park, there rose a deafening clamor which turned all well-lubricated heads in its direction. In a half sober V formation, the People's Park wheelbarrow of myth, coupled with some twenty angry people, rushed the stage. At the head of the V was Joe Smith, park regular and driver of the rock-filled wheelbarrow. The wheelbarrow tipped over and palm-sized pebbles filled the dance floor where, seconds ago, dancers were getting their groove on. The crowd surged forward, each of us grabbing a lucky charm from the pile, as the cops looked at each other like the Three Stooges just before someone gets bonked.

There is no prettier sight in the fight for freedom than the retreat of cops in full riot gear. A few rocks were thrown, but for the most part, it was a scowling match rather than an armed conflict. We formed a barricade to hold the park through two days of tear gas, truncheons, and the free pizza donated by true believers everywhere. After many long hours, the Mayor of Berkeley negotiated a truce.

Days later, I walked by People's Park and saw that same wheelbarrow being used to clean up the debris from the melee. I saw Joe Smith sitting on the grass, nursing a brew, and dozing off. I asked him what his plans were now that he was out of jail. He looked at me with his troubadour of trouble smile and said: "Refill the wheelbarrow and plug in a band next Sunday!"

It took six more years of refilling that wheelbarrow before the UC Regents capitulated and allowed monthly concerts in People's Park. By then, Ronald Reagan had been elected to a second term in the White House. Free Speech is like the wheelbarrow: If we can't defend our right to Free Speech with common garden tools, what kind of flowery words will the next generation of rebels have to plant in the soil of People's Park?

40th Anniversary Of The Free Speech Movement (FSM)

It's such a simple thing when you think about it. We have these minds, vocal chords, our spirit, and the will. Together they spell FREE SPEECH. Oh sure, it's in the US Constitution, and some sort of nod is given to the right to air our grievances, via the courts, mass media, or at worst, reality TV shows. But let's face it; these are mere words on an empire's lip. A bike is not a bike until you learn how to ride it. Wherever you are on the planet, there is a battleground for an unspoken truth yet to be told. It was a mere 40 years ago that a group of Cal students came back from a summer of voter registration in the South. As they set up tables to tell their stories and organize for the fall, they were told to pack up their leaflets, their right to Free Speech, and shut up.

The first amendment is a "you don't know what you have 'til its gone" kind of issue. Free Speech seems so easy to understand, but so hard to put your fingers on. Amidst the shifting sands of public opinion and regional interpretations one can be lost at sea with nothing but words to float your boat.

FSM Sather Gate

FSM 40th - Top of Car

Julia Vinograd, the Bubble Lady, at the FSM 40th

FSM 40th UC Berkeley

BERKELEY POLICE BLOTTER

DESCRIBE CHARACTERISTICS OF PREMISES AND AREA WHERE OFFENSES OCCURRED.

Plaza area located on university property.

DESCRIBE BRIEFLY HOW OFFENSE WAS COMMITTED.

Suspect was in the center of a large crowd yelling, shouting obscenities and disturbing the peace of students, faculty, and staff preparing for final examinations. Would not cease when ordered by police officer.

DESCRIBE WEAPON, INSTRUMENT, EQUIPMENT, TRICK, DEVICE, OR FORCE USED.

Mouth, voice.

OBJECTIVE – TYPE OF PROPERTY TAKEN OR REASON FOR OFFENSE.

Personal satisfaction.

WHAT DID SUSPECT SAY – NOTE PECULIARITIES.

"Fuck the pigs", "Nazi", "Gestapo pig".

VICTIM'S ACTIVITY JUST PRIOR TO AND/OR DURING OFFENSE.

About lawful business.

TRADEMARK – OTHER DISTINCTIVE ACTION OF SUSPECT.

Political activist known for disturbing peace on campus.

DECADES MAY COME AND GO, but some of Berkeley's most prominent citizens keep up their good work, and provide a steady frame of reference in these troubled times.

Stoney in the Daily Californian, 1980

POLICE BLOTTER

DESCRIBE CHARACTERISTICS OF PREMISES AND AREA WHERE OFFENSE OCCURED

    Plaza area located on University property

DESCRIBE BRIEFLY HOW OFFENSE WAS COMMITED

    Suspect was in the center of a large crowd, yelling, shouting obscentities and disturbing the peace of students, faculty and staff preparing for final examinations. Would not cease when ordered by police officer.

DESCRIBE WEAPON, INSTRUMENT, EQUIPMENT, TRICK, DEVICE OR FORCE USED

    Mouth, voice

OBJECTIVE - TYPE OF PROPERTY TAKEN OR OTHER REASON FOR OFFENSE

    Personal satisfaction

ESTIMATED LOSS/VALUE AND/OR EXTENT OF INJURIES - MINOR, MAJOR

    N/A

WHAT DID SUSPECT SAY - NOTE PECULIARITIES

    "Fuck the pigs", "Nazi" "Gestapo pig"

VICTIMS ACTIVITY JUST PRIOR TO AND/OR DURING OFFENSE

    About lawful business

TRADEMARK - OTHER DISTINCTIVE ACTION OF SUSPECT

    Political activist known for disturbing the peace on campus.

THE DAILY CALIFORNIAN

VOLUME X, NO. 221   THURSDAY, JANUARY 3, 1980   BERKELEY, CALIFORNIA

Stoney celebrates 10th year in politician-bashing business

By Ralph Jennings

There must be something "outrageously funny" about Stoney Burke – his weekly political satire on Dwinnelle Plaza draws a bigger crowd than most campus protests.

Burke, who drew about 400 people to his commemorative presentation last Friday, said he has satirized political events for 10 years in the San Francisco Bay Area.

Burke spoke at length about the November presidential elections (1992). If the Bush-Quayle ticket wins, Burke said, "Bush will be in the bushes looking for casual users of life."

But he added, "1,000 points of light . . . that's Dan Quayle on acid."

A member of the audience asked Burke if he planned to run for president in 1992. "I'll be running from the president in '92," Burke answered. Burke also commented on baseball.

"The whole story of the World Series was drugs," Burke said. "Cortisone won."

Asked to comment on the future of the United States, Burke said, "There won't be enough to eat, but you'll still have to wash the dishes."

Burke also showed an hour of his new video, titled "Stoney Speaks." The video shows Burke attending and satirizing the 1984 Republican convention, the Pope's visit to San Francisco and the Navy's return from the Persian Gulf.

The video also shows scenes of Burke visiting his native town of Romeo, Michigan.

"My dream is that every channel will be Stoney," Burke said after showing the video.

Burke also presented two Berkeley poets, Julia Vinograd and John Michael Jones, in honor of National Poetry Week. Vinograd and Jones read their poetry, in which they criticized U.S. society.

The audience reacted favorably to Burke's presentation.

"I heard the ring of truth there," said Avery Colter, a UC Berkeley student.

"It's vital that people like him speak their minds," student Dustin Tranberg said.

"He's just outrageously funny, and definitely on the right – I mean left – side of politics," said Michelle Yaichka, a "concerned member of the community."

Burke said people in Berkeley can expect to see him perform for a long time.

Hunkered Down In Berkeley

My sleeping bag is painted the color of the sky and coated with a stealth lining. This is what I'm hoping as the sun drips into the sea, splashing bright reds in the sky to signal the end of this known day. I have never made total friends with the night. When you have no shelter, the darkness can hide you, but never comfort you. All sorts of events are in store for you if you choose to, or are forced to, wander the streets at night. Not the least of those dangers being the local guys in blue, who need to see your official papers. Someone who's had their innards kicked backward out of society needs to account for oneself, even in America. In Berkeley, nature was always my best friend. There is the humongous and beautiful Tilden Park just to the east of the city of Berkeley. Its many forests and heavily scrubbed terrain are perfect for disappearing in. One can never thank the evolutionary forces enough for giving us the trees to hide under, and shelter the unwanted. Someday the DNA-twisting white coats will invent a tree that points a leafy LCD light at your sleeping place for the local rousting militia to move you along. Until then it is in their arms we nestle. And it's a nod to the Great Spirit at the end of a long day.

Stop The War

There was a day, not that distant in the past, when a Marine recruiting table set up in the morning at a college campus would certainly being drawing protestors and street debaters to thrash the subject of WAR around a bit. This picture best describes the feeling of people who, for one reason or another, just missed the Vietnam War, and were in no hurry to have the next generation get caught up in endless military adventures with vague objectives. Sound familiar?

These US Marine recruiters are getting pretty much the same welcome they received some 30 years later in downtown Berkeley at the Marine recruiting station. Who will stand up to the war machine as it grinds our kids into McWar burgers!?

Marines' Table 1980

The Tale of Two Helens Art Sale

One was of another age, much before my time. The other way ahead of my time. A curve of learning was to be had with both that would last the rest of my life. I'm talking ART teachers here

I grew up in a small-town farming community. Sports, God, and Work – in that order – was the breakfast of champions. I tried never missing a day in school, because that's where there were books, ideas and friends. Helen Starkweather of Romeo was the art teacher long before I realized that art could be a way out of this mind-numbing jock culture of the Midwest. Ms. Starkweather was a small woman with a stoop and a refined vocabulary. She had a grumpy cheerfulness about her that made her of another era altogether. Old and old school.

I thought Art, Home Economics, and Shop were all one major, until I met Helen Starkweather. I can still hear her voice ringing in my ear, "How do you know you can't do it unless you try?" or the dreaded, "Show me what you've been working on." She handed out paintbrushes to kids who were just off the farm, and to Jocks just off the basketball court. Eminem is always pouting about how tough it was at eight mile road. Hek, we were all the way out to 32 mile, with only Helen Starkweather and an empty canvas in front of us. When Helen passed she willed her house and studio to the Village of Romeo. There her spirit lives on in all creative work that goes on in her studio, to this day, because art is forever. And don't you forget it!

Historic Moment

We fast forward to the untouched canvas of a sunny day in Berkeley, California, where I am waiting for Helen Holt to finish her shift at the UC Art studio right underneath Biko plaza. On this day she is going to show me how to research, cut, and design images to go with the text on my free handouts. Helen had her own edgy take on the onset of the Reagan era. Once she helped organize a performance group called EZ TV Demolition. This performance entailed six people dressed in hazmat suits driving a van onto campus with a TV set in tow. At a given signal the TV is placed on the ground, smashed with sledge hammers, and just as quickly swept up in a trash bag, an hustled quickly away before the police could arrive. Onlookers were subliminally induced to smashing their own TV's at home. By day Helen was an Art instructor, by night she was the refrigerator lady on KPFA's "Over the Edge." We had a short but fantastic run as the performance band Historic Moment. Helen went on to design art lamps and play in music jams whenever she can.

An American In America

As a kid growing up in Romeo Michigan, I would never have dreamt that I'd return there as the star of a documentary film about – ME! Nor could I have dreamt that as a adult, I'd get kicked out of my old high school for being too political – something I managed to avoid in the waning days of the 60's. Back then, the War in Vietnam raged on and on, and the protests mounted. By the time I graduated from Romeo High School in 1972, the war was winding down, and I was assigned a lottery number instead of a possibly one-way trip to boot camp.

But life is strange, isn't it? Not in a straight line, off to the side, a "bend around a curve" kind of flow to this life. When I was a kid, canoeing down the Rifle River with my dad, every bend and ripple in the river was a new adventure. One turn of the corner flushes out a giant Blue Heron, or a hidden log might tip the canoe. But you keep going. Life is like that.

My life is certainly like that. There I was, the Principal in Swedish filmmaker Kage Jonsson's "An American in America." My general show business strategy has always been: Hit 'em high, hit 'em low, go fishing, and follow baseball in the middle. This strategy has absolutely failed to bring financial success. The riches I have mined are the mind-spinning grins, thick with gooey adventure, which most certainly can be cashed in at the end of the day for a great story.

I first encountered Kage Jonsson and his crew in San Francisco, at Fifth and Market, on a sunny day in 1979. I was raging on in a most engaging way about Jimmy Carter's big teeth, and the Coca-Cola corporate stains on his bib. The SFPD were just wrestling me off my soapbox when a Swede with wild eyes and a bouffant of gray hair stepped forward to try to calm the situation. On this day I was lucky. The SFPD preferred I "move along," and Kage and I became fast friends. Before long, he had hatched an idea for his next award-winning documentary – "An American in America."

That day, Kage followed me to a local comedy club. There he posed the advance-three-spaces question: If you could do anything you wanted to right now, what would it be? I answered as best I could: To do what I do now all over the country, and get paid for it. The traveling sage, the raging son of my Uncle Sam, the verbal equivalent of Woody Guthrie's smashing-Fascism guitar. My wish was granted, and the result is forever on film. But like any project, this one has a side story of many events that eluded the pan of the camera.

One afternoon in Memphis in 1980, down on Beale St., was just such an event. Kage and I had dropped by the Blues Museum to inquire about an "authentic" blues musician for a scene in the film. The curator was quite helpful, and told us to wait at the café across the street. Within an hour, a spotless red pickup with plenty of chrome to roam swept into the street. A very large black man wearing a cowboy hat and dazzling gold chain strode into the café and over to our booth. I immediately recognized him as Albert King, one of the greatest blues guitarists of all time. Of course, Kage and the crew had no idea who this flamboyant man was. I tried to explain, but perhaps too discreetly, that without this man's music, Elvis Presley would still be driving a truck. Unbelievably, Kage said that he was looking for a smaller, and maybe poorer, blues musician. What?? Mr. King was not amused.

The next day, we drove through Cloverdale, on Highway 69. The scars of the Civil War are still visible in the green fields and on the Delta, which has given birth to that uniquely American sound. The Blues.

It was in this film that I returned to my hometown. My father and mother had their big scenes, and later I went back to my high school to be bounced from campus. I got to relish peeving off anyone I might have missed in high school.

When the school officials found out I was pontificating about the draft, unemployment, and everything else I could think of, they promptly asked me to leave. Just before I go, one of the administrators sputters one of the best lines in the film, "Where are you going to run and hide when the Russians come over here?" Ummmm... Romeo?

An American In America

The Advisor Newspaper May 14-20, 1980 A-3

Stoney stirs trouble
"Up against the wall – "
By Ed Bas, Associate Editor

Romeo High is still spinning from the enigma of Pat "Stoney" Burke's visit to his old alma mater last week. Burke, now 25 and living on the west coast, is described as something of a character by teachers who knew him. And at least one teacher and high school principal David Olson is a bit upset with Stoney for his return to Romeo last week. Olson said Burke "misrepresented" himself

On Tuesday, Stoney showed up at the high school, said "hello" to Olson and a few of his ex teachers, and asked for permission to film on the high school grounds. Olson said he was led to believe, or at least assumed on his own, that the film was to be of Stoney giving a mime demonstration, something he had been involved in as a youngster.

Olson even cooperated to the point of lifting a few students out of Mary Eberlines art room to sit in as "extras" and the kids were happy to cooperate with the Hollywood atmosphere, although it was reportedly a Swedish film crew.

Once outside though, Stoney reportedly began to reintroduce a bit of 1960's-style campus activism. Olson said it was straight out of Berkeley, and you could almost hear the strains of Jimi Hendrix in the background. When Eberline dropped by to listen in, she found Stoney telling the students they were being repressed by society at large and by their own school and teachers. "You're all going to be drafted and go to war in Iran when you turn 18," Stoney reportedly told the students. He went on to blame the school's government class and even the required reading, stopping just short of calling for a revolution.

Most people smiled when they re-told the story, not so much angry with Stoney or his actions but peeved with the way he did it. Olson said he felt used, and said he wouldn't have minded Stoney organizing a protest or talking to students off of the school grounds. As it was, he practically invited – although unknowingly –Stoney, and even helped provide an audience.

Olson said he would even consider suing if the school or its students were used in a false light.

Near as anyone can tell, the film crew was filming Stoney's return to Romeo as biographical material, possibly for some sort of promotional campaign.

Eberline said she was worried that a few students might have been swayed and even asked a few to discuss what he'd said in case it bothered them. On Wednesday, Stoney was reportedly off again for parts unknown – "the south" someone said. Some people at the high school figure his visit lasted long enough.

So You Want To Be A Free Speecher?

Why not? Won't cost you a dime, just a little of your time. Here's a simple guide, to take you on that first amendment ride. Yes kids, do try this at home.

1. Have something to say.

2. Find your spot.

3. Wear something different.

4. Bring a friend.

5. Bring a box or chair to stand on, be loud and proud of the first amendment!

6. Find a current newspaper, and a noise maker too.

7. Speak as if people are listening, even when they aren't.

8. Know your rights to minimize legal hassles.

9. Be sincerely outraged at just about anything that has happened to you in the last 24 hours or 24 years.

10. Don't give up, and keep a schedule to prove you are going to be there…until whenever…

SoapBoxing it's the new craze, get up on it.

Don't get off it. Up and down, 'til the system falls.

Stoney For President

Every four years I run from the president. And any election year I will fling fractured promises on the walls of history, kiss babies, and raise enough funds to keep me in touch with my special interests. Although my platform has morphed over time, there are some basic points that I try to put forth, year after year.

1. If there is a minimum wage, why is there not a maximum wage? Let's put the stopper at about $200,000.00 a year. If you go even one penny over the maximum, you are flung back to a Spartan-like existence starting with a personally monogrammed sleeping bag and a corporate-sponsored shopping cart for all your things. Makes balancing the budget as simple as old math on the farm.

2. If we can send little robots to drive around the red planet Mars, we can invent a slower bullet. Guns are the only consumer product where death is the moniker of a success. If used as intended, it will kill consumers. That's just wrong. We need to develop a bullet that is no faster than an electric wheelchair or a 10-speed bike. For Pete's sake, let's give people a chance when they are shot at. If you can't duck, roll away, or dance the crazy two-step, what hope is there for humanity anyway?

3. If we have cable TV 24 hours a day, why can't we keep the libraries open for 24 hours a day? Let's throw in a folding bed that can be used as a bridge to the dream world to sort all the worlds in our mind. Isn't it the dream that morphs from books that we read, that bring us new ideas to live or love, or survive?

4. Professional athletes would be paid on a diet of daily merit. Every home run would be worth $100, a tackle in the end zone is an extra-large pizza. Nascar car racing, the skill of turning left for two hours – an obscene waste of fuel – would be digitally transferred to a friendly neighborhood demolition derby website at a library near you.

5. Each citizen gets two pairs of shoes. One for themselves, and one to know how the other person might be faring in the world.

6. The twenty-dollar economy. Everything costs 20 bucks, everybody that you know has 20 bucks, everybody always owes you 20 bucks. Thus at all times, you will have 20 bucks in your pocket.

7. Washington, DC would be put on wheels and moved to Kansas City, MO. This way we don't go broke trying to redress our grievances with travel costs. Let the government come to us for a change.

8. Your vote will come in the shape of a Frisbee. Every four years you take a shot at the person who is most likely to catch the Frisbee. In the case of a recount, it's just a flick of the wrist.

9. To discourage the very rich from whining endlessly about how hard they suffer for their greed, a digital wealth bubble will float over their heads during any appearance on TV. For instance, a one-hit pop star worth $150 million who flippantly complains that he is bothered by paparazzi and too much fame would have his digital bubble flash wildly until he acknowledges the struggle of working people who are not part of the fantasy 1%.

10. An end to automation! Soulless machines that don't have to eat or crap are getting all the best jobs. There's nothing wrong with pumping gas for a living wage, if the darn machines would give us a chance. Next thing you know they will charge tuition for online college courses where you never have to see or talk to a person. Oops, they already have that.

Live Wild Or Die

RECALL   STONEY FOR GOVERNOR   RECALL

I hearby declare that government itself must be recalled
for funnelling money and resources
into the senseless destruction of Mother Earth.
The masters of the black sciences continue to direct their R&D
to comical yet highly dangerous games like a
Nanotechnology center here on campus.
How about using the money to train and fund
thousands of real LIVE teachers,
instead of micro homeland security robots
patrolling the "FREE" skies of the continent!
As governor, I would put People before Machines
. . . let the green earth bloom again.

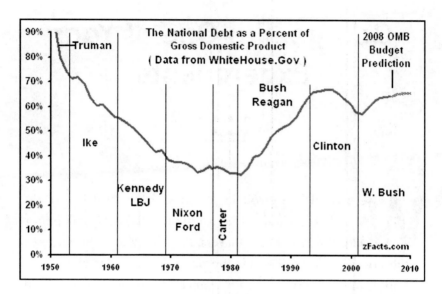

National Debt

Ronald Reagan Hood

George, I'm One of Your Experiments

We arrived in Detroit in August of 1980, just before the Republican National Convention, and quickly set up shop with the Plutonium Players, Pat Halley, and the Rattones at the Frieze Theater. This was the place, in the heart of the Cass Corridor, where everyone had a chance to perform for the Lefty Choir, find solace amongst fellow travelers, and make new friends.

We found out that WE were to be the loyal opposition who were expected to stare down the GOP machine. At this time in history, security was very light compared to post-9/11 America. Your credulity might be strained, but these things DID happen. I have been a fly on the wall in many odd places, but in this case, it was like someone left the window open, and the honey jar uncovered. So, here we are, on the first day of the convention, trying to find a sleight-of-hand, satirical way to make up for being in the land of no laughs.

A solution presented itself when we found a program of "Special Events" sponsored by the GOP, one of which was a youth rally at Cobo Hall. We couldn't let the big suits and upper-ups off that easy, could we? The Pentagon's secret heat-seeking Clown Detector had yet to be invented, so I was safe in my sad-sack clown costume. We removed our political buttons and all obvious outward signs of intelligence or free thinking, and blended right in. I did, however, keep my handy bag of noisemakers, plastic flowers, and rubber chicken. Like Charlie Chaplin's accidental Communist, we were swept along by the parade of Reagan Youth, chanting "USA! USA! USA!"

We came to our senses when two well-dressed Party Hacks appeared with giddy agendas and maxi-glee faces. One was holding a magic clipboard, and the other was nearly collapsing under a load of Republican picket signs. Clipboard Guy was barking orders to volunteers, while Sign Guy was distributing his signs. With big smiles, we accepted our signs and learned the new chants before agreeing to be conservative, yet peppy in support of Governor Reagan. We marched, like the 600, into the darkness of the auditorium.

Inside the beast, I could barely maintain my Stoney-faced composure. Tossed by waves of smiling youth on a sea of blind enthusiasm, we saw a list of speakers that read like a menu for secret societies and dark conspiracies. There was John Connolly, the man who had suffered the "lone" gunman's bizarre buffet of bullets as he silenced JFK on a sunny afternoon in Texas. There was George HW Bush, head of the CIA who bullied his way onto the Republican ticket. And there was Jack Kemp, the football hero throwing long on the septic field. During the cold-cut-sandwich-like speeches, the huge crowd was so disconnected from the speakers that they were confused about when, and for what, they should applaud. By the time George HW Bush mounted the podium, we had perfected the gradual crescendo to wild applause at parts of his speech which were meant for quiet reflection. The rest of the crowd followed our cue, and the ripple effect sent an odd message to the candidate on stage.

We worked our way to the front row. As GHW Bush tried valiantly to ignore me, I whispered "George, I'm one of your experiments." At that time, there was a lot in the media about mind-control experiments which were conducted by the CIA under Bush. At first, he tried to ignore me, but when I took off my hat to reveal a full head of bright green hair and whispered, just a bit louder this time "George, I'm one of your experiments," he began to scowl at me with malice. He seemed to think that

something more than one of his experiments had come back to
haunt him. In the middle of his speech, George Bush pivoted
away from the lectern, and the house lights came up a bit. The
gray suited, earpiece guys materialized all around us, and rather
politely, asked us to join them in the lobby for a chat. After deny-
ing any affiliation with any deviant group, and claiming that we
were only in need of "refreshments," the nice agents said we could
leave if we promised not to come back. We did, and we did.

Dr. Kissinger, Hart Plaza, And My Friends At The ACLU

I t was a long, long ride from San Francisco to Detroit. My ever-faithful friend, trivia expert, and keeper of the flame Michigan man RJ Tincknell stuffed in the back with Little Ritchie of the Hog Farm and me. A couple of Plutonium Players up front. We were bound and determined to give our own special welcome to that greasy-headed cowboy, riding backwards into the sunset ... Ronald Reagan.

DAY 1: I stood at the bottom of the escalator, blue haired and baggy saggy pants. Henry Kissinger drifted down the grinding metal escalator. Roy Cohn, red haired and satin suit – the dark hand of McCarthyism – was patting Henry on the back, smiling, throwing off the occasional bizarre laugh. A green, haunting mist enveloped them both as they floated down the steel steps into my Cheshire grin. I greeted them both at the bottom of an oddly unguarded escalator. My spiked blue hair and oversized shoes probably screamed out "Hired GOP Clown." I grasped Dr. K's hand and pulled him ever so closer to my fun house mirror face, and said quite firmly, "YOU ARE THE BIGGEST FASCIST OF ALL." Before the period was put on the sentence, his security goons elbowed me to the ground, and crammed their bloated client into the mouth of a waiting limousine. My assistant RJ tugged on my sleeve for a quick exit, and we melted into the night. We were wise to put a hop in our step, and a retreat back to the Frieze Theater. This was the first day of the convention, and so far it was playtime in the school yard, with no hall monitors in sight.

Political conventions, like mayflies, last a very short time. Each day is filled with another adventure in the corporate fantasyland of the 1%. Although each party tries to shield itself from dissent and chaos, there is usually an understanding that some sort of fenced-in corral is set aside for a "counter convention." When one strays from the cage, danger lurks, and the police are quick to ratchet down. On one given day, I naively thought I could just speak "anywhere." My lawyer friend George Corsetti, Ishmael Ahmed, and I decided to go down to Hart Plaza to exercise our free speech. Hart Plaza, with the Dodge fountain's cool spray, seemed like the perfect place. When we arrived we quickly realized that a rope had been strung around the public space and the GOP had red, white and blued the entire area for its corporate master's picnic lunch. I was dressed just as colorfully for the occasion. My prop box was opened, and my voice was tuned to a sweet, but dissonant tone that was to be expected when my class enemy has me trapped between the Detroit River and the first amendment. Trying my best to be funny I start with my best material. Q: "Do you know what Reagan means by supply-side economics?" A: Put the supply on his side and forget about the rest of us!" So far so good! I nervously continue. I try another. "Did you know that if you take the name RONALD WILSON REAGAN and switch the letters around a bit they spell INSANE ANGLO WARLORD? I'm on a roll now. "RONALD REAGAN loves America so much he wants to create two of them, the rich and the poor!" The seething conventioneers have had enough anti-HA from me, and promptly call the police. I'm cuffed, roughed, and carried off to jail. On that day I can thank George and Ish for having my back. The GOP strong arming of the first amendment repulsed them as well. They promptly called the ACLU, who called the local Court officials, who immediately called the GOP front office, and said in no uncertain terms: "It is grossly unconstitutional to arrest a citizen for exercising their right to free speech on public property."

The GOP opined that they had rented out Hart plaza, a public park, and could thereby restrict speech to their whim and wishes. When Ishmael and George came to spring me from jail that day, they were accompanied by an ACLU lawyer who led a cowering, high GOP official on a tight leash made of a thousand regrets and a "it won't ever happen again" apology. Over the years people have asked me why I don't add more lawyer jokes to my arsenal. It's like the "Ghostbusters" theme song, "Who you gonna call?" A comedy crowd at the club with a two-drink minimum? I don't think so.

Yippies, Reagan, Abbie And Lennon Die

Following the Democratic convention to New York City I found myself part of the Yippy world of the lower east side. I was their guest, and enjoyed being introduced to the "Pie man" Aron Kay, Dana Beal, Dean Tuckerman, and the whole cast of characters I dare not expose. One day we all went to a park near the Statue of Liberty to protest the appearance of Ronald Reagan and his wife Nancy. We tried to hoist our "REAGAN FOR SHAH" picket signs, but a wildly hostile crowd surged to threaten us if we did.

On another day we all marched down to courthouse to see Abbie Hoffman just after he came back from hiding. We took over some seats overlooking the balcony, and unfurled a banner which read DON'T BUY THIS BOOK, a takeoff on his famous book entitled *Steal This Book*. I stole that book, way back then, and hitchhiked the USA with it in my back pocket.

One of the fun things I was tasked to do was call up Electric Lady Land studios in NYC where John Lennon was recording and plead for fundraising assistance for the Yippies' various causes, including a new café down on Bleecker Street. I never got past the reception desk. A few months later John Lennon was shot down in cold blood by some whack job who had a Jesus problem. America was just too much, with too many guns. I took leave to Europe, where Reaganism was akin to that which occupied them in WWII.

Fix-It-Yourself Theater Lyrics, Amsterdam, 1981

LET EL SALVADOR BE EL SALVADOR

let el Salvador be el Salvador
the junta is our friend
and we'll back them to the end
try to fake some elections
we only have good intentions
we're the generals of big business
the fantasy on your TV
we're marching into other lands
just so that you'll be free

CORONATION DAY SONG

the banks were burning
the cars were turning
and we really had our day

chorus:
Let's krak the palace
and send her to Dallas
who needs a queen anyway?

she has three houses
while I have none
my roof is leaking
and I'm on the run
you get your crowbar

I'll get my tools
we'll krak that palace
and live like royal fools

NO RELIGION ISN'T COMING

chorus
no religion ain't coming
no religion ain't coming
we've got to think for ourselves
until those funeral bells
so live and love as you please

they say there's going to be some big big changes
a rumbling of the earth and sky, well
don't ya fear, the end isn't near
it's only the fool in your eye

they say they have the golden key
and life could be so fine
just follow me
and I'll set you free!
and you'll find it's all a crime

no we don't have the answer
we don't know the answer for you
we'll just take your questions
but won't give suggestions
so live and love as you please

chorus

holy, holy, holy
all the money's piled high
everybody's happy to die

A Fool In Amsterdam

"So let's krak (squat) the palace,
And send our Queen to Dallas.
Who needs a Queen anyhow?
She has three houses
while I have none ....
and we're, we're, we're
... on the run!"

Those were the words that "Stoney Burke and The Fix It Yourself Theater" sang night after night in village, hamlet, prison, or youth center in Holland in the year of 1981 as part of Amsterdam's "Festival of Fools Festival." We had our final gig as a performing group in Vondel Park. The Dutch Government actually gave our ragtag bunch of actors/ squatters/rebels a grant to tour the land for the better part of a year. Here I am, overstaying my visa, talking all kinds of smack about Reagan's USA, singing anti-monarchy ditties, and teaching theater to folks in a squatted (or "KRAKKED" as they would say in Dutch) building. That's an ally giving the baby boomer American kid an anti-Nazi break. Thank you, by the way.

After the release of *An American in America,* I had this brilliant (not) idea to take the only two reels of my nascent film career and head off to Europe – the land of the lefter than left of where I'd ever been before. Reagan had just been elected. A stinky, dark, supply-side theory vapor had descended on the land. In retrospect, perhaps it would have been wiser for me to stay in the USA, and

immerse myself in the "let's do it for the Gipper" folly unfolding.
That regret has passed. I never could have replaced the education I received that year busking in Amsterdam. Nor the elation
of performing at the open Bak in the prestigious public theater in
Amsterdam. Something so evil was riding backward cowboy style
into the American sunset that it was impossible to stay in the USA.
I gained a whole world perspective on what other people thought,
lived like, and struggled for in the process. Nothing like travel to
warp speed, fast forward an education. You cannot put a price on
that. Once you leave the shores of the USA, you quickly come to
terms with the vapidity of our TV/commercial culture. You are
forced to defend it, the good, the bad, the silly, whether you liked
it or not. While I was still wondering who shot JFK, the USA press
overseas was salivating over, "Who shot JR?"

The first few months of the long Holland winter, I slept in master juggler Dr. Hot's old van that was parked right alongside of the
Prinsengracht canal. An eerie, cold blue haze would creep up on
the old cobbled streets of Amsterdam and snake its way along the
canals to little pubs with Dutch literary names. No matter how few
guilders I had, or how little Dutch I could speak, I could be part
of that that great city. I was a regular performer of sorts on the
Leidsplien. I'd have my spot, a place to be, where I'd meet more
lifelong friends like Gary Auslander and Caspar Oudshoorn. I'd
eat and live on whatever few guilders I could scrape up. I busked
relentlessly on the streets of Amsterdam, but I'd hardly call myself
a successful one. Just like back in Berkeley, the best friends I've
made in life I met on my spot, doing my "stoney" thing. A few
guilders here and there, and the flowers in Vondelpark, and the
zest for adventure kept me high and away from world of want.

My theater group came from all walks of life, never made a
dime and worked like the dickens to make our sqautters unit the
best it could be. There was Robbie, who wrote all the music, and
Marga who sang sweet harmony and translated my bad Dutch into

song. Later on Reint, who had never acted in his life but had a natural born clown face, would lope around the stage with his gangly goofy build, and get some of the biggest laughs we ever had. The wind would howl outside our drafty squatted theater, as one troupe member had to watch the door for the police or immigration. After a few hours of rehearsal we would disperse back to our cafés and squats and agree to meet again soon. The next day I would by chance meet up with Gary when he tired of writing his novel and head over to Caspar's favorite cafe, Jan Hueva, for tea and talk. There were times when Caspar would drum up a kale, sausage and potato mashup that would get us through to the next day. Back then the next day was all we had.

The Fix It Yourself Theater, Amsterdam
(Featuring Stoney in a suit!)

Festival Of Fools

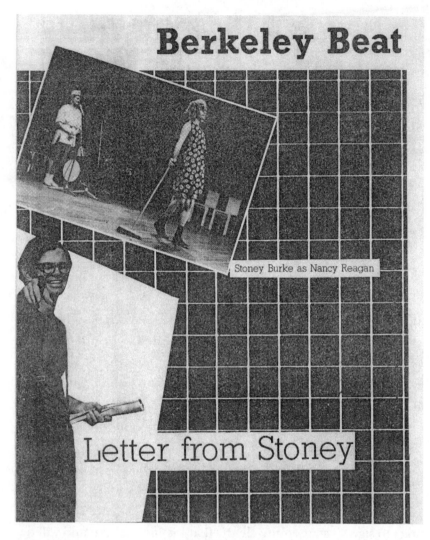

Berkeley Beat

Stoney Burke as Nancy Reagan

Letter from Stoney

HELLO AND DAG UT,
Someone sent me an article you wrote recently and I thought I'd write
and let you know what I'm up to these days. I started out in London in
August, then to Scotland, Berlin, Frieburg and then finally Amsterdam
since September. It's been a hard year for me here, as I can't use so
much English, and my . . .

I Was Thrown Off The Wally George Show

Wally's Hot Seat, Los Angeles, California, 1980s

Back in the Reagan era, I made many trips to Los Angeles, California. I was one of millions who either hoped to be discovered at The Comedy Store on Sunset Boulevard, or just dreamed of being seen by a talent agent who might happen upon me and one of my crazy shows at UCLA. A group of frat boys that hung out on Bruin Walk had forwarded my resumé to the father of combat TV, Wally George. Wally wasn't just a right-wing, conservative TV host. He brought the genre to levels of vitriol that his mentor Joe Pyne would never have dreamed of.

I had been prepped by people in the know on what to expect. The first thing you did when you arrived at his TV studio was wonder why you agreed to do this in the first place. His studio was located smack dab in the middle of Disneyland's parking lot. After shaking hands with Wally, his legal staff corners you with a contract to sign. It states quite clearly that his "police" can and will do you physical harm if the HOT SEAT needs ejecting. I knew that was not going to happen, so I signed on the dotted line.

Finally, the red light on the TV camera comes on in the studio. His rabid, flag waving audience is foaming at the mouth. WALLY! WALLY! WALLY! Several audience members are out of their seats and making menacing hand gestures in my direction. I was the "liberal wacko meat" they had come to eat from Wally's table. In his half-hour show, there were three segments. In the first he set me up for the second. During the commercial break he takes me aside. His snarling persona morphs to sweet. He explains how in this next segment, I say this and he says that, and then we both come close to blows.

After the commercial break we come back for the third and final segment. He had this whole phony scam worked out in his head. I'm from the Pete Seeger School of say "yes" to whatever the producer wants you to do – until the cameras are rolling, and then you do what you came for. Wally's combed-over white hair, cold blue eyes, and frothing peanut gallery has me on edge. Quickly into the second segment Wally starts berating me, "I bet you are one of those sick liberals who are in favor of illegal immigrants taking over America?" I take along hard stare at the picture of John Wayne on the wall behind him. I'm thinking about this "consent to remove physically" contract I signed. Finally, after a few moments of mock disgust at the question, I reply, "C'mon Wally. Both you and I know the only illegal, un-American people on stage are YOU and I. The Native Americans are the only ..." I had not quite finished the sentence when Wally jumped up out of his seat and screamed to his audience, which had been worked into a throbbing gristle of hate, "THAT'S IT!! You're out of here! Go back to UCLA and your disgusting, scumbag, communist friends!!" With that his "police" marched forward to grab my arms. I raised my fist, waved them off, and jitterbugged to the exit as comically as I could.

I waited in the green room for the show to end. Here comes Wally all grinning and warm like a mortician who just got paid. "Why don't you come back next week?" he asks. I say "Sure, why not?" I never did. Wally was running a scam of fake hate, and that's the worst kind. Wally George is gone now, so I will not speak too poorly of the dead, only to say, I wonder who's on the hot seat now.

THE DAILY CALIFORNIAN

BERKELEY'S INDEPENDENT DAILY – ESTABLISHED 1871

VOLUME XIX, NO. 53   THURSDAY, OCTOBER 30, 1986   BERKELEY, CALIFORNIA

USF jails Stoney Burke during Nazi bombing threat

By Brian Hill, STAFF WRITER

Comedian Stoney Burke, who regularly performs for lunch-hour crowds on the UC Berkeley campus, took his routine to the Jesuit University of San Francisco yesterday and was jailed on suspicion of involvement in a white supremacist bomb plot.

Burke, whose routines include such quips as, "This is a melting pot all right. The scum rises to the top while we get our asses burned on the bottom," said he was performing in an Uncle Sam suit at noon on the campus when the campus police asked him to leave.

Minutes earlier, at 11:50am, an anonymous caller had told campus police that five bombs planted in two buildings would explode within an hour, said USF public safety director Joseph Costello.

According to Costello, the caller, who yelled "Heil Hitler," and "save the white race," said the bombs were placed "in retaliation" for the presence of too many foreign students on campus.

Burke was performing in front of one of the two buildings mentioned in the threat.

Burke said the campus police approached him and told him he did not have permission to speak on the private campus. "Some guy asked me if I was a communist," Burke said, "And then (the policeman) grabbed me and said you have to get permission."

Costello said, "At that point, we didn't know what we had on our hands. We got a call of disturbance in front of the building where an individual making political pronouncements of some-kind was asked to leave and refused to do so."

At that point, Burke said, "They started dragging me off, and everytime I got my hand free I started yelling."

You're Wavy Gravy, Aren't You?

A sunny, beautiful day. On a hill just above the fog line sits The University of San Francisco (USF). It's a Jesuit University on the fringe of the sunset district in San Francisco, California. If you are a local, you'll know the location as the point at which the fog decides to stay where it is, or if the wind is right, go full-bore into the city. This day was not a fog day. The air was sea fresh, and the sun bounced off the white marbled neo-gothic cement of the oldest buildings.

More often than not, in the early days of my speaking adventures, I'd try to expand my territory. I'd try just about any school that I could get to, and that I had a political gripe against. Ultimately, my showing up at a private Catholic college to pontificate about my secular vision of the world would be fruitless, but adventuresome. Even though this place was in San Francisco, my idea that gold should be left in the ground, and no one should be forced to their knees would be a tough sell. The words "Private" and "Catholic" would ensure that I would probably be accused of "Trespassing" and "Heresy" before the day was through. And, should the Campus Police opt to remove me from campus this sunny day, none of this Free Speech mumbo-jumbo would work on them.

The Hell with caution! The Pope be damned! Life is short, and the Gospel According to Stoney must be disseminated! My clown nosed is polished, and my mind properly bent!

As I prepare myself in the lavatory, I am resplendent in my powder blue, oversized polyester pants. My old referee shirt is tucked in nicely. My green spiked hair glows in the sun. I wonder if the priests get the same thrill as I do, just before the big sermon. On this day, there will be no mistaking me for a choir-boy commie, or an ultra-pious anarchist. Hek, before this day is done, I just might confuse, amuse, and inspire a few of the students to think for themselves. Nothing more, nothing less, game over.

Getting a speech started is the toughest part of any outing for me. There is no advance publicity machine to grease up the expectations, no opening act to tag-team the inevitable rejection. There is just me, with froth-mouthed rabid verbal assaults, rat-tling off the unpredictable stream of ideas that flood my twitching mind. Getting all worked up into a satirical word bath is what it's all about. It's high noon on the Plaza. It's Stoney Time.

Having been raised a Catholic, and having strategically flunked out of our town's only parochial school, I felt uniquely qualified to release a load of genuflecting bile on some Holy Father's pol-ished penny loafers. Here goes nothing. My voice goes from quiet conversation to crazed, as I launch my attack on these gold-plated Cardinals. The Catholic Church's missionary position on absti-nence had the students laughing already, but before long, even the cautious by-standers are coagulating into a mass of cheers and jeers. Here I am, jousting on the home field of the Knights of Columbus, with no visible resistance! Just as I think this is all going well, I notice there is something strange happening on the other side of the now-encircling crowd. The doors to the surrounding buildings have been flung open, a fire alarm is wailing, and stu-dents are pouring out into the sun-filled Plaza. I'm standing in the middle of the whole student body, a chorus of alarms singing, with the uneasy feeling that something very odd is taking place.

This could be a REAL emergency, so I stop what I'm doing, take note of my surroundings, and put a cap on the trap until I can find out exactly what is going on. No sooner had I taken my vow of silence, when the Campus Police drive up with a full set of Christmas lights twinkling madly.

When the Campus Police roll up, they leap from the car,

clumsily handcuff me, and toss me into the patrol car like a sack of red potatoes. This is not looking good to me anymore. Granted I know I can stir the passions of the ever-present word Gendarmes, push some buttons, get the dust flying, and at least test the limits of the local Free Speech ordinances. But this? For God's sake, someone must have put in a call to the Vatican itself! Did someone report that Damien was in the Quad telling jokes and spitting pea-soup with his horned headpiece on?

I did not find out until later that the Nazis had called in a bomb threat.

In the patrol car, the two cops are looking very nervous, with much fidgeting and growling into the two-way radio. After a short ride around to the back of the Administration building, I am hustled down some stairs into a holding cell. I know better than to say anything while in custody. The wearing of clown clothes, and the gleeful spouting of heresy on the Quad might be unusual, but I get the feeling that my creative use of Scripture for my own revolutionary agenda is not the real problem here. Play it cool and meditate.

I can tell by the way the Police keep staring at me through the bars that I am the prime suspect. There is a way that cops stare at you before your lawyer arrives that is supremely unsettling. After a brief discussion, one officer suggests that they call the San Francisco Police. As police will do, as you stew, they discuss in front of you your fate.

"Maybe SFPD can tell us more about this guy, his motive, and what charges we can file," one officer sneers at me, while talking to his partner. I didn't like this one bit. All kinds of things can happen during Transfers To Proper Authorities.

In walks Sergeant Wilson, of SFPD. He looks like one of those "lifers" who would have no problem hooking me up to a blood sucking machine that would drain my vital resources into some lawyer's greedy veins. After a moment of private conversation with the Campus Police, Sergeant Wilson saunters over and stares at me. His head twists slightly, like a golden retriever trying to understand Sanskrit. He points to my suitcase filled with props, masks, and, of course, my medicine. He says, "Is that yours?"

(Gulp) "Yes," I answer.

You see, my cool, meditative veneer is beginning to crack, because I have just remembered the ping-pong sized BUD I was holding for a friend. This cop would have to be blind to miss it. Damn. Now it's not only trespassing and disorderly conduct – let's throw in possession, too. I'm thinking of cutting the ultimate Catholic deal. Just let me go back into the sun, and I'll genuflect endlessly on the Quad, and refill the holy water jugs the rest of the semester. The Nuns would never let that slide, but maybe Sergeant Wilson?

With another in a series of angry scowls, Sergeant Wilson grabs my bag and disappears into an outer office. Five minutes go by. Then ten. Yup, right about now he's found the crime, written a report, and is calling for the meat wagon to drag my bones from the shadow of the Vatican's boot camp. Game Over!

After an eternity, Sergeant Wilson returns with my suitcase. Very deliberately, he sets it down, straightens up, and looks me in the eye. I see his knowing grin and shudder.

"I remember you from the sixties," he says. "You're Wavy Gravy, aren't you?"

I just look at him, not sure what to say, but starting to think I've happened upon a bit of luck. I summon every trick in my good-scam playbook, and slowly build my quiet fear into a feeling of triumph. Careful not to say yes or no, I smile beatifically, like the clearing of the fog over the Golden Gate. It was the look Sergeant Wilson wanted to see. He laughed, and winked like he was in on the joke.

"This is not the guy you're looking for. He would not do such a thing."

The Campus Police blush. Frustrated, they quickly uncuff me. Sergeant Wilson hands me my case, and soon I'm back outside. ALL of my belongings were right where I'd left them.

Uncle Sam Goes
To The Psych Unit

Uncle Sam (yours truly) was taken to the psychiatric unit during the 1984 Democratic convention in San Francisco. At the time we thought it was Orwell's *1984* we were living in. A B-grade actor took over the presidency and gave every right wing idiot a wild ride on the back of his imaginary "back how it used to be" jalopy. San Francisco was hosting the convention of the other band of corporate brothers, the Democrats. This year of 1984, they were countering with Walter Mondale, of the famous Monotonous family. Was this just another creepy SF Noir film?

Here's how my story goes. A friend who I did not know left a security pass in a phone booth. I just happened along wearing an Uncle Sam costume for reasons I could not fully explain to the Secret Service. I then gained access to the 1984 Democratic Convention using my super-secret, 3D, sparkly security pass. I proudly strutted in wearing my ragged, but royal-looking, Uncle Sam Costume. Ragged you ask? I am the long lost nephew of the real Uncle Sam. "I want YOU to bring the Troops home," was my battle cry. Too many wars have left my proud suit in disrepair. "America! Put the guns down, and come out with your heart open!"

I was supposed to be reporting on the convention for Pacifica radio station KPFA. Instead, I was lurking in the shadows of another superhero free-speech adventure. I walked briskly around the whole of Moscone to find out what would be the best spot to let loose with the word. I figured if you are going to face the cold steely grip of justice, it's going to have to be worth it, rhetorically speaking. My topic to the convention? "Homelessness." Or as we say on the street, "Kicked butt backward into the sand-trap soup of despair." I found the irony in the displacement of the displaced to make way for this convention of supposed progressives. It would be worth it.

Governor Mario Cuomo of New York was set to give the speech of his life, and so was I. Of all the states' seating sections, Nevada looked very empty. I gambled on the element of surprise, hubris, and guts to get a jump on my oratory leap into the jaws of the law. I crawled over velvet rope and stood on a chair. After taking a deep breath, I looked around at my puzzled audience and launched into my rat-a-tat-tat of statistics – a tale from the heart of the haves vs. the have nots. The homeless in San Francisco were forced to give up what little they had so that the happy talkers on the "left" could gather in comfort. No sitting here. "Move along" was the familiar tune played by city officials.

My voice was raising now. I was standing on the chair. This was no time to have nothing to say. Careful not to use any naughty language, or aggressive gesturing, I was within a normal kind of crazy, or so I thought. I was about five minutes into my oration, when two suits show up to wrestle me off the chair.

Soon I'm doing the Gumby dance as a pair of handcuffs bends my arms up and backward. A small crowd has gathered now inquiring about all the commotion. The two security agents are eager to find a hole to hide me in. A cub reporter, with cute little notebook and pencil, steps in front of the two grey suits with me in tow. "Where are you taking him, and what will happen to him?" A very good question, and quite timely I thought. One grey suit turns on the reporter and growls diplomatically, "Don't worry about a thing, we're just going to ask him a couple questions and let him go." The reporter shrugs, mumbles "OK" and wanders off. That would the last time I heard from the press until I was released 48 hours later. So much for the follow up question! We three, the two agents and I, load into an elevator and make our slow descent into the bowels of the Moscone Center.

It is in these moments that you call on all your spiritual resources to pull you through this ride into the sticky fingers of the government. Meditation is a healthy outlet for relieving stress. In this case you get small in your physical body, moving your mind and spirit into the bunkers far away. Finally we get to the agent vs. suspect interview.

Agent: "Are there any presidents that you like?"

Uncle Sam Stoney: "I really liked Richard Nixon. He did the best job on the country, or as far as he could go."

By the look on the face of the secret service agent, I knew that would be the last joke of the night. Before I knew it, the cold steel of the handcuffs clicked shut, and I was hustled off to the nearest exit into a waiting unmarked car. I suppose I should have been flattered that no less than four agents were assigned to escort me to wherever they had planned to take me. Slow night for clowns in cuffs I thought to myself. All four agents' faces seemed to blend in with the steel and cement landscape that swallowed the night.

First stop is San Francisco General Hospital. After I am securely handcuffed to a chair, the agent steps into an office to consult with the night nurse. I can see him gesturing and pointing at me as he explains the chronic symptoms of Uncle Samism to her. I finally get my chance to explain just what the hek is going on when the nurse comes over with her clipboard and a quizzical look on her face. We clearly had a cultural disconnect when she fully admitted she did not know who Uncle Sam was, much less Stoney the clown. The fact that the Democrats were having a convention a few blocks away was lost on her. Soon I was once again in the backseat of the grey Lexus with the four emotionless grey suits for travel mates. We merged onto the Bay Bridge, hugging the rail side of the water at high speed. I still did not know where we were going. As the car suddenly slows down, the agent in the front passenger seat starts loudly fiddling with something in the glove compartment. I'm saying nothing, hiding deep inside myself and dreaming of Ocean Beach on a sunny day. We are now crawling at 25 in a 55.

"You know ... we could stop right about here, and throw you over the side Uncle Sam. Who would care?" All four agents are staring straight ahead, poker faced, not a hint of a grin. A cold, clammy sweat starts working on my chest. My Adam's apple was now the size of a bowling ball. Swallowing air was so sweet. The two agents in the back seat must have rehearsed flexing their muscles at the same time to put the death squeeze on my now caving chest. By the time the car exited the bridge, I was convinced I'd never see my Mom and Dad at Christmas again. I was never so glad to see a psych ward in my life. Unlike our last stop, the doctors at Highland Hospital were none too convinced I was guilty of anything but a fashion crime. I was held for eight hours on a 5150 charge, and released to the warm embrace of my Frog house friends. About two weeks later I received an invoice for $500 for my own incarceration! I never paid that bill. That would have proven I was crazy. After all, I was just Uncle Stoney on a mission to speak at the Democratic Convention in the year of 1984.

Stoney loses opportunity to make 'keynote speech'

By Laurie Goodstein

Two secret service agents handcuffed and detained Uncle Sam at the Democratic National Convention Monday night, cutting to 30 seconds his address on world peace and freedom of speech.

"I didn't want (N.Y. Governor Mario) Cuomo to have the only keynote speech," he said.

Local comedian Stoney Burke walked through convention police barriers wearing a red, white and blue Uncle Sam suit and a green convention security pass, which he later told police he "found in a telephone booth."

The political satirist, who often performs at UC Berkeley's Sproul Plaza, was detained for four hours and subjected to psychiatric examinations, first at San Francisco General Hospital and later at Oakland's Highland Hospital. Burke said he was not permitted to call his lawyers during his detention.

According to the police report, Burke shoved someone as he was pulled down off his soapbox, a chair reserved for a Nevada delegate. Burke denied that he pushed anybody.

Burke, who estimated he has been arrested 12 times, said he was released after a doctor at Highland Hospital determined no psychiatric treatment was necessary. "The doctor went to bat for me," Burke said, "once I told him I didn't wear those clothes all the time."

Stoney loses opportunity to make 'keynote speech'

Two secret service agents handcuffed and detained Uncle Sam at the Democratic National Convention Monday night, cutting to 30 seconds his address on world peace and freedom of speech.

"I didn't want (N.Y. Governor Mario) Cuomo to have the only keynote speech," he said.

Local comedian Stoney Burke walked through convention police barriers wearing a red, white and blue Uncle Sam suit and a green convention security pass, which he later told police he "found in a telephone booth."

The political satirist, who often performs at UC Berkeley's Sproul Plaza, was detained for four hours and subjected to psychiatric examina-tions, first at San Francisco General Hospital and later at Oakland's Highland Hospital. Burke said he was not permitted to call his lawyer during his detention.

According to the police report, Burke shoved someone as he was pulled down off his soapbox, a chair reserved for a Nevada delegate. Burke denied that he pushed anybody.

Burke, who estimated he has been arrested 12 times, said he was released after a doctor at Highland Hospital determined no psychiatric treatment was necessary. "The doctor went to bat for me," Burke said, "once I told him I didn't wear those clothes all the time."

— Laurie Good⋯

Stoney Does Dallas
1984 ... GOP Convention

• • • •

Not long after I was released from the custody of a Secret Service hold in San Francisco, I managed to scrape up enough money to follow the counter convention events down to Dallas, Texas. This time I was joined by my old friend Bob Hercules and his steady ready cam to film "Stoney Does Dallas." This episode was followed up by "Stoney Does Houston" in 1992. Both are excellent renditions of the circus we call political conventions, inside and out.

For the most part it's the counter conventions outside that not only are the most fun, but hands down the most highly relevant events in the choosing of the next president of the United Mistakes of America. The fire ants at the camp site near the convention site drove most attendees to seek higher ground elsewhere. The little red insects had a bite that reminded everyone there of the pain Ronald Reagan Hood could inflict by robbing from the poor to give to the rich. All with a nostalgic Gipper wink. We came to call this Zen fascism. Bob and I had no problem gaining access to the half-empty convention Astrodome to get our camera shots. Dave Whitaker was the MC on stage at the concert site at night, while the NO BUSINESS AS USUAL coalition did nonviolence resistance and sit-ins during the day in the financial district.

After a blistering week in the Texas sun, even the horny toads had given up and gone home. But not the Yippies, grey panthers, and anti-war groups that came to Dallas in the summer of 1984. Finally, on the last night of the people's stage, a historic concert to let the GOP know that Ronald Reagan's second term would be just as undesirable as his first. Headlining the stage that night was one of the best anti-fascist punk bands of all time, on any continent.

The Dead Kennedys! I was slated to co/MC the stage with veteran movement maestro Dave Whitaker. I can remember jostling with him over the microphone to be the one to introduce The DK. It's true what they say, nobody wants to hear a comic speaker while a band's amps are humming and ready to rock. Nevertheless, Dave and I both insisted on the honors. In the end I deferred reluctantly to Dave. He was, and still is, the elder statesman in modern-day revolutionary America. As a limping Jello Biafra ripped thru a bevy of their now epic hits, there came a signal offstage. The moment we had been waiting for had arrived as planned. There was a security blunder only Dallas officials could explain. All of the delegates were forced to exit the Astrodome right next to the stage where the DK had turned the dusty field into a tornado of mad mashers. Several hundred delegates were made to shuffle nervously past the stage with only a chain link fence separating the two groups. In one voice, with fists in the air the cry went up FUCK OFF AND DIE! The chant echoed late into the night, and long after The DK left the stage.

Reagan was reelected as it would be. As for me, I felt much like the twist in an old song the DK had refurbished: "I fought the law, and I won."

Dead Kennedy's Handbill

Sleep-In

A few movements ago, and two decades ago, there was a vicious and oppressive system of racial segregation called Apartheid that soured the country of South Africa. Nelson Mandela was imprisoned on Robben Island for 25 years for his part in the struggle to rid his country of this fascist by-product of WWII. Many corporations and prestigious Universities were called upon to divest their complicit "DeReagan, DeKlerk. DeNazi, all DESame to me."

Although the issue seemed like a no-brainer, many people went to jail across the USA, trying to incite change in US policy toward South Africa. I was a student at San Francisco State at the time, and to say that students were taken up with the cause would be an historical understatement.

There is a 30 day sleep-in at Stephen Biko Plaza at UC Berkeley in 1986. Notice the banner which indicates the number of nights spent camping out. Twenty-five years later, the UCB police sent 50 riot cops to stop OCCUPY CAL from setting up a mere three pup tents.

Not long after the street battles of the '80s had subsided, and South Africa was rid of apartheid, Nelson Mandela spoke to a capacity crowd at Oakland Coliseum. He was on tour to thank people for helping end apartheid. There was not a dry eye in the house as he delivered his victory speech. I was there that day. I saw his freedom dance. I heard his words of hope.

Photo: Dave Blackman

Sleep In

Photo: Dave Blackman

Vonnegut Talks III, Biko Plaza

Photo: Dave Blackman

Pep Rally On Steps To Bilko Plaza

Dave Whittaker / Diamond Dave
Activist, poet, and occupy camper, Dave takes his turn on the soapbox
just down the street from Occupy San Francisco.

Occupy Or Die

L ike a storm that needed to happen, Occupy Wall Street burst onto the scene like an SUV on a wild ride through the garden of money and up on to the curb of the 1%. The power surge of people was incredible. It was like the rush of an errant wave at the beach. You never quite expect the tide to reach that far on shore, until it does. The Black Bloc contingent was oddly named, as it is mostly white kids living out their smash-the-state fantasies. Whether one likes it or not, they have moved the discussion from nonviolence to crimes against property. In theory, this sounds like an appropriate response to the police violence inflicted on the Occupy movement. And for the most part it is. But here's the catch. The movement grows slower, more cautious, and fearful. Who gets to decide when a building is trashed instead of squatted?

I am committed to nonviolence myself. It is easier to break something than to build it. Easier, and weaker, to shoot than to talk. The robot culture is still befuddled when the humans just don't cooperate with authority.

Is the issue the cops or the politicians that hire them? Is it the forest or the trees? The General Strike in Oakland, CA was a glorious affair for the most part. The direct action of taking over the streets of a city, of pushing the automobile mob to the fringe of a massive demonstration against corporate greed, is empowering to say the least.

If anything, the great recession of 2008 has give us a language to speak in. There's the 1%, and there's us the 99%. Or is it that simple? The authorities have lowered the bar on just exactly where you can occupy. Back in the 1980's the students at UC Berkeley occupied Biko plaza for 40 days and 40 nights. In 2011 a police riot broke out on exactly the same spot when students tried to erect three pup tents. Four days later 20,000 students packed the plaza to re-Occupy their own campus.

All in all . . . when you have nothing, you occupy what you have. And what you don't have, get ready to put a coat of paint on it, sweep the floor, and keep a-going.

Occupy is not over. It never will be. Once you realize you have nothing and nowhere to go, you are, as Dylan says, "Napoleon in rags."

Occupy U.C. Berkeley

Stoney in Pig's Mask

Bernardo and Stoney

Stoney with rubber chicken under Sather Gate

Swami X

Down Upon The Swami X River

I can still see him now, bent over his newspaper on the steps of Martin Luther King Student Union at UCB in Berkeley, CA. When I stepped foot in Berkeley for the first time in the late '70s, I came with a mime's white face, no voice, and a suitcase filled with dreams. For me it's been more like a long college course in mutinous diatribes than a Tinseltown pipe dream.

One of my early teachers was none other than the legendary Swami X. On some days, after he was through, he'd walk up the plaza to check me out, laugh, do a shout out, then wander back down the hill not to be seen for the rest of the day. For all too brief of a time we hung out together, smoked weed, and traded paranoid visions of the world. One time we piled into his old beat-up Cadillac convertible and streaked down Hwy. 101 to Stanford University. A special Swami X blend of red haired bud that he broke out for a special trips would leave an exhaust trail all the way back to B-town.

At Stanford we'd take turns standing on the tables in front of the cafeteria, trying our best to outdo each other in front of the gawking, walking, apathetic, and disturbingly conservative frosh.

I realize now he was handing me keys to his ranch. Places he had performed for many years in Northern California were pointed out to me. It was going to be up to me to tend to the garden of the eternally absurd. Places that to this day have never seen him again and perhaps never will again. No ticket stubs or underground posters to catch the Swami X moments gone before, or wax nostalgic upon. Such is the history of street speakers. A life under the radar of the money-making machines. But right in your face when you walk the streets of America.

On the way back from our trip to Stanford he paid me one of the highest compliments a man of his stature could summon up. He said, "Stoney, I think you are being used by the CIA to test the limits of free speech, to see just what you can get away with and what they have to watch for."

His remark *did* refresh my memory of a time about three years previously at the University of Oregon. For a quick $50 I let the psycho lab hook wires to my skull, a thermometer up my ass, and a thermal gadget to my pulse. For the next two hours they showed me car crashes in slow motion, bunny rabbits with stiletto heels for ears, and an old newsreel of Hitler in a dress walking backwards. But that's another story.

I was humbled and flattered at his observations and the time he spent with me, which in retrospect was like being accepted into a world where the odd must be honored and the obscene can be the ripe fruit of folly.

The year was 1978, and shortly after that Swami X moved south to Venice beach, where he continued his raps on the Venice beach boardwalk until his retirement. Despite some effort on my part, I was never to see or contact him again. I would hear from the rumor mill of his doings and whereabouts. Nary a show of mine would go by when one of his many denizens would say, "Where's Swami X?"

I often wonder how retirement suits him, if he misses those glorious days in the sun under his sombrero cranking up the crowd for the coins that would surely flow his way? Wherever you are Swami, there's always a spot for you in my circle, and bless you for being so damned noncommercial.

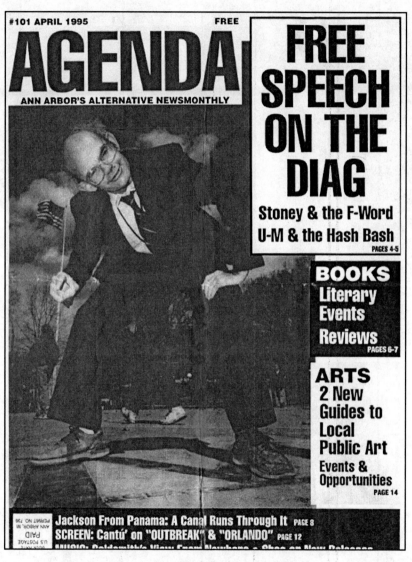

Free Speech on the Diag

He gets arrested a lot, and people marvel that he can support himself by passing the hat after each impromptu performance. But that's life when you're a

Street-corner anarchist

By TOM FITZGERALD
NEWS SPECIAL WRITER

Stoney Burke wants to fight this noon. Hunched over like a monkey, he scampers back and forth, dangling long skinny arms that are dark with hair.

"You maggots!" he screams, then licks his lips. "You scum. Somebody take me on. C'mon! C'mon!"

Students, gathering on the steps of the University of Michigan Graduate Library, don't know what to make of him. They shift their backpacks, sip soda pop, laugh uneasily.

A tall, curly-haired man wearing an orange-sleeved shirt steps into the Diag and crouches in a karate stance, edging forward warily. Abruptly he stands up and, smirking, unzips his fly.

"Oh, that's it!" roars Burke. "Go below the belt. Go for your Cruise missile." Then he's off on an obscenity-filled tirade against superpower politicians who want to blow the world up with nuclear weapons to prove their machismo.

The crowd is swelling. Newcomers stand on tiptoe at the fringes. "Who is this guy?" they ask. "Is he on drugs, or what?"

Burke's sweatsoaked shirt won't stay tucked into his baggy trousers. His bright yellow tie looks like it glows in the dark. Peering from behind round, owlish glasses, Burke searches the Diag for a target.

An Army ROTC student in dress uniform makes the mistake of strolling by at that moment. He stops to see what the commotion is about.

"Hey there, soldier! What you fightin' for?"

"So you can be free to stand out here and bitch about everything," the officer-candidate says. Applause. Stoney is burned, and he knows it. "Bull . . ." is all he can say.

But he quickly recovers. "Are you going to be an officer?" Yes. "Have you been to boot camp yet?" No.

"Aw, that's too bad," Stoney says, zeroing in. Then you haven't met the enemy yet. The poor guys from the southeast part of the country who can't get jobs anywhere else so they go learn how to kill people. Man, they're going to do the fighting and dying in El Salvador or somewhere while you sit back behind some sandbags and map out coordinates."

Burke, a 30-year-old street comic with radical political views, has been haranguing Diag crowds for about a month now. He came from the plaza at the University of California-Berkeley, where he and his invective had become fixtures.

A native of the Macomb County community of Romeo, north of Detroit, Burke was in southeast Michigan to visit his parents, but got restless and decided to work. And now he *has* to hang around — he's got a November court date in Detroit on charges he disturbed the peace in September while "performing" at Wayne State University.

He's freewheeling and frequently obscene. Burke improvises from newspapers, magazines, a few props, the behavior of passers-by. He often doesn't know what he's going to say next.

It's a living. At the end of each performance — two or three a day, depending on how he feels — Burke sets his felt porkpie hat on the cement and asks the audience to toss in money.

□　　　□　　　□

Stoney's sitting in a booth at Eden's Deli, 330 Maynard. He rakes a huge pile of coins toward himself like a winning poker player, then starts piling them neatly by denomination.

"Somebody dropped in a 10 today. God bless 'em," he says. "People say, 'How do you make it?' I make it because people believe in anarchy, in revolution, in change."

Burke believes in all those things — and more. His big crusade of the moment is nuclear disarmament.

"Why I'm here has to do with bombs and making people aware that here in their campus community there's military research going on," Burke says. He often uses humor to urge students to fight against that research.

"I'm really just a little guy shouting, and not 500 feet away some scientist in a white frock is making a cruise missile or some other genocide weapon I didn't get to vote on."

He believes in civil disobedience. On more than one occasion, he's told his Diag audience it would be a good idea to "take over a building" to protest military

See ANARCHIST, D2

The Diag
University Of Michigan
Ann Arbor

The big cast iron M is implanted square in the middle of one of the all time best outdoor speaking spots in the USA: The Diag, at the University of Michigan. A place of debate, study, and the start of every protest march. From the Hash Bash to the last student party. Like birds on a wire, the terrible townies, preachers, and comics offer up an animated buffet of humanity. All on just one little square.

The Diag, where the First Amendment means something. I should know, having been dragged off of it, and applauded for being on it. To me it all means something.

The Diag, a place where even the cops are antifascist and will not run you off for "language that could likely lead to violence." At other schools and in other cities, this means every utterance this side of passing gas.

There are stories to tell, my friend, and I make a long journey to stand on a box in the middle of the village and speak out for those who have no voice on the secrets of our times. To have my lungs fill up with the fresh air of freedom, to hear my own booming dissident voice echoing off the bricks in the plaza, these are the stories to tell. Riding the range, wildcatting a public space and taking it over for an hour or so just to see how the show goes. Maybe be back next week, or maybe the NeoCons are taking the

Frat Boy jokes too seriously.

Hey, did you hear about some of the most popular frats on campus? There's I FELTA THIGH, I DRANKA KEGGA, and I SIGMA MEANS NOTHING! Doing all of this with no beer sponsorship is quite refreshing.

Catch me if you can!

Stoney debates a conspiracy theory at the University of Michigan 2010

My Time At
The University Of Michigan,
Fall 2012

My first day at the University of Michigan in the fall of 2012 was not on the preferred first day of classes. It was September 6th. I have a home 72 miles from Ann Arbor. One has to play the percentages with traffic and weather to be on time and in the thick of Diag free speech. The rain and the ensuing traffic chaos made the first day of classes a no show. Perhaps it was all for the better, as day one was a Greek recruitment day on the Diag. Yeah, it's one of those kinds of schools. Public and private get murky, mixed and insidious. Who knows what sort of trouble awaited me there? This being the third day of classes, it was another mega "disorientation" event called Festifall that I had to contend with. This was where every organization/student group in the entire university had a table on or near the Diag. Just about every sidewalk and open space was dedicated to this event, except for the steps of the Harlan Hatcher library at the south end of the Diag.

The Harlan Hatcher Library, which houses the Labadie Collection on the 7th floor, has the largest curation of 19th, 20th, and 21st-century Social Movement history. My old and dear friend Julie Herrada has been the curator for almost as long as I have been pontificating on the steps below.

I'd prefer to NOT attempt a diatribe under these circumstances, but the shrinking wilderness area of free speech dictates

that you take the days you have and make the most of it. This year
I have designed a new END OF THE WORLD robotic toy theater, and printed up several dozen placards that I clip on a poster
board to explain my robot's motivations or sentiments. It is what
I call the triple threat theater – there's my mouth, the robots, and
the placards (for silent running). Before the day was out I would
need to employ all three to avoid the police-like "staffers" who
seemed to have a nifty list of rules they had made up special for
this event. In short they read like this, "You are not a student, leave
the area or we will call the police." It is the first phrase authority
figures learn in "How to Hassle the Townie 101."

All of my theater is loaded onto a lil' red wagon that I pull
along. I make several rounds around the Diag area to see just
where I might fit in, or muscle in, as the case may be. I finally
end up in the only legal/logical place to rant and rabble the day
away with humor and significance. Lo and behold, and not that
surprising, a whole pack of born-again evangelists have beat me to
the spot. Now my back is against the Bible and the civilian "event"
staffers. I can't let a bunch of Jesus-hates-everybody stink talk rule
the free speech area. I am compelled by a higher authority than
you or I to intercede. And besides, if they can speak, so can we.
Right? It's as simple and legal as that. Or so you would think. Later
in the semester. This charade with the cops and the "events" people went on for weeks until about one week before midterms.

Photo: Mark Brunner

Keshia Thomas shielding KKK member, Ann Arbor, MI, 1996

File this under, "I was there!" I get a lump in my throat when I think of the depth of humanity it took to save this KKK guy from a fate unknown. This woman not only believed in nonviolence, she personified it this day.

Word Cops On Patrol

Maybe you know the kind of day I'm talking about. The air is cresting the big 60, winter is on the wane, and the Diag is bristling with anticipation. Something spontaneous just might happen. On any given day I may or may not be one of those events. Even that assumption can trip you up. The weather was prime and the people were there to hear some slagging on the Government. So just as I have for the last 15 years or so, I put on my baggy pants, painted my hair green and strolled up to the Diag to unload.

Just about the time the GOP rumbled onto the scene to finish off the Democrats last November it was time to hibernate for the winter. But today was different. It's high noon now and you have to start somewhere. Somebody yells out "Stoney . . . what do you think of Newt?" "Fuck Newt Gingrich!" I say it loud enough so that the MTV casting party ambiance is rippled but not concerned. There's always the chance that no one will listen. Unfortunately a young, but heavily armed, UM policeman is listening. Meanwhile I'm letting even more steam off about Gingrich. I'm just starting to warm the voice and roll the words off the tongue.

"You cant say that here. Pick up your things and come with me!" I heard his voice and met his glare. Yet, I felt I've done this all before, at just about every school I've spoken at. The same command and stare. I've spoken on the podium at the Republican convention, as the host of my own TV show, and as well on the campuses of University of California at Berkeley and the University of Michigan. Each venue has its own peculiar set of rules. Free

Speech in my twenty-odd years of experience can be as unpredict-able as Michigan weather.

The officer motions towards my performing box and he repeats the command. I inform him as calmly as possible that the Constitution gives me tacit permission to critique the powers that be. He's not buying the free speech rap at all. Starts twisting his neck and talking into his radio. I'm thinking this could be a long day with another Trial of the Century to bore people with for the next six months. He's done talking on his radio and starts demanding some ID. He wants to see if the green hair is pictured on the license. My head says I should cower and comply. My body senses that I might have a better go of it if I just start doing a crazy dance.

The crowd is getting bigger and the laughs are starting to come. Meanwhile the Word Cop is announcing that if I won't give him my ID, "He'll just get it himself." Now I guess that he's audition-ing for an episode of "Cops." About 200 people are watching him search my bag of tricks. He seems pleased as punch when he finally finds the wallet containing the ID. When he finds the actual ID, he removes it like it's state's evidence. Now another officer shows up and stares at me for awhile. Probably hoping I'll say that word again.

While the officers are waiting for some reinforcements, time is of the essence. Now I'm working the lungs overtime hoping I can gather the Diag together for the moving blockade off campus. Three years ago at Oregon State University the students took over the administration building until the cops set me free. Wow, noth-ing describes the feeling of . . . getting away. Would this be one of those days? I keep talking, trying to make a desperate situation interesting.

These are tense moments. No knowing whether the riot squad is hyped to go or maybe Dr. Thundersplatt is searching for a more reasonable solution to the Word Crime. It's in these moments that I flash back to all the great times I've had on the Diag. To stand tall when you know you're right, to face off with the conservative twats on their own turf, that's what the Diag means to me. I'm not about to let some rookie security guy fence me away from the cheapest and I think most cosmically connected online facility there is: The Diag. Out under the blue sky with my feet firmly planted in mother Earth. And by golly I'm going to hold my ground and maybe some other people will too.

"Let's put those mountain bikes to good use by building a barricade because I am going nowhere!" I shout. The tension is doubling in a funny sort of way. Now I'm counting six cops. More desperate jokes. What do you say when that might be all you are going to be saying for awhile? Now I'm getting mad knowing that I have to go back to work (cab driving) with no license and who knows what charges. Word Cops cruising the Diag. Just like they will be surfing the internet soon. I find out later that if there had been women and children present they would have pressed charges. Like what is this . . . lil' house on the prairie Diag? I mean what century are we living in? People have a right to protected speech in the Diag for Pete's sake! Shouldn't there be a Free Speech area in every city, village, and farm where people who can't afford to go online can voice their opinion?

So now the cop conference is over and the offending officer offers to give me my license back. I say, "Why don't you put it back where you found it? I never gave it to you . . . remember?" Now he's in a jam. He can't very well just put it back with the same nonchalance that he took it with. Finally he says, "If you want it, come down to the DPS office to get it." With that, all of the uniforms leave. There I am, tangling with the Word Cops on my first day out. Anything after this is anticlimactic. I manage to joke that, "Those officers and I travel around the country performing this word search-and-seizure circus. How'd you like the show this afternoon?" I am exhausted, must go home and call lawyers and the media. I decide to go down to DPS in the morning. Trouble can wait.

In the morning I am riding my bike down Dipke (find that on your map drivers!) to retrieve my Drivers License. Out of DPS comes the veteran officer I had seen the day before at the Diag. He yells behind me as I ride by, "Hi Stoney! Everything's OK. You can pick up your stuff in there." I smile. The spirit of the Diag comes through again. People ask me all the time why I speak at UM and UCB. Mainly for the simple reason that I can. And you bet I am going to continue to do it. As I tucked the DL back into my wallet and rolled into the hot sun, I thought of all the times I didn't get away. Too many stories to tell. This one is among one of the sweeter tales.

The day following the return of my license I attended my first-ever drug-test orientation meeting up at the Yellow Cab office. The pink, wrinkled face of Ronald Reagan flickered spookily from the video monitor. He sternly reminded me of my right to remain silent while the Feds took the piss out of my bladder and the words out of my mouth. As I sat listening to the plan to ship my urine to Utah for testing, I couldn't help but wonder, "What will it take to get our right to privacy back?" In the end, it will be up to us. And as a result, there is one place I know of where you can say "Fuck Newt Gingrich!" and be pissed off at the same time. The Diag!

Shakey Jake

Shakey Jake was a street legend in his own time to anyone in Tree Town, USA (Ann Arbor, Michigan). To Shakey's fans, it would come as no surprise that he is in the street performer's hall of fame. Or will be if we ever build one, that is. Everyone else has one, why not buskers? That's what makes busking so great – financial success means not having to busk anymore.

Shakey Jake was much more than just a character who dressed odd and walked around with a guitar. There are plenty of those. Shakey embodied all of the elements of an urban legend. I remember one bitterly cold day in February, the temperature was five degrees below zero. I was in my warm, comfortable taxi, tooling down State Street, there he was on the corner, dressed like a cosmic layer cake. He was holding his guitar upside down and wildly strumming a tune written just for this glorious winter day.

"Hey, Jake!"

THANKSGIVING WITH JAKE

[1996. Directed by Dave Chappell. Cast: Stoney Burke and Shakey Jake Woods. Ann Arbor Community Access Channel 9. 30 mins.]

Truth be known, if Ann Arbor had to choose a holiday meal with anyone in town — including mayors, sports coaches, university presidents, and others of that social ilk — there's not much question who'd be at the top of the short order list.

Now through the courtesy of Stoney Burke's fabled cable access program, *Stoney Talks TV*, two of Tree Town's most gone of gonzo warriors are available for dining with Ann Arbor — Thanksgiving-style.

Stoney Burke interviewing Shakey Jake Woods has more than a lot of potential going for it. We're not talking Martin and Lewis, here. Nor Clinton and Dole, for that matter. No, this has more sizzle than King Kong vs. Godzilla.

Jake, Ann Arbor's resident street philosopher and bluesman extraordinaire, is the perfect guest for Burke's incisive guerrilla-styled reporting. In fact, the best thing about this priceless documentary of future local folklore is Burke's surprisingly low-keyed handling of the ever-volatile Woods.

For Jake — who comes across here as a dynamic blend of 4/4 superstar and Dear Abby — is enough of a personality to hold any audience's attention. And Burke allows Jake the crucial space he needs to hang out all-over while smoothly manning the community-access call-in phone lines for the many callers who prostrate themselves with fervent abandon at Jake's feet for advice from Ann Arbor's hardest working singer/songwriter.

Serenading his television audience with original riffs (some cooked up on the spot) and a select blend of traditional cover tunes, Jake takes the time out of his busy schedule to set Ann Arbor's younger and older folks straight on what ails their lives.

In their quite earnest take on the meaning of Thanksgiving charity — and, more crucially, why we should enjoy it — Shakey Jake Woods and Stoney Burke both reaffirm the meaning of the true holiday spirit.

You, too, will walk away singing the graces of *Thanksgiving with Jake* after spending a little off-season turkey time with this dynamic duo shaking down the tree during America's most privileged national time-out.

• •

Diag character stony Burke: more than 'just plain silly'

Burke goes mouth to mouth with Preacher Mike

By Ben Deci

The limelight of Ann Arbor's street scene has a limited capacity. There is tough competition to join the ranks of such local notables as Preacher Mike and Shakey Jake.

But now there's a new name on the Diag. Stony Burke is easily identifiable by his outlandish duds, his dyed hair (green, red or blue depending on the day), and his political orientation. Stony took time to talk about himself during his typical speech warm-up: a falafel from Oasis. In contrast to his Diag style, Stony was soft spoken and very polite – he didn't even speak with his mouth full.

Stony was born in Romeo, Michigan in 1953. Although he often singles out the educational system for sarcasm, he is himself a graduate of the University of San Diego.

It was on the West Coast that he began his career as an orator some 15 years ago. He has spoken out on campuses across the country ever since, amassing quite a following, especially in California.

Stony described himself as a political satirist. "My views tend toward the left, he said. "My message is for students not to give up their political beliefs in this cold world atmosphere. We need to try to make this country the best it could be. I preach revolution. Oh yeah, one more thing," he added. "Peace."

As Stony began to perform, his soft-spoken voice was transformed into a growl, and he punctuated every point with a tailor-made string of profanity. A campus safety officer circled as Stony's audience began to grow.

Officially, only organizations with University affiliation are permitted to set up on the Diag. A spokesperson for the Student Organization Development Council said the council could investigate or have a person or group evicted from the Diag if they received complaints.

One person who may complain about Stony's activities is Preacher Mike. Stony takes a decidedly anti-evangelist stance and has taken over the role of chief heckler during Preacher Mike's sermons.

"I've got to get this show started before Preacher Mike takes my spot," is his typical opening line. He can often be heard protesting the "monks with guns" that terrorize the Diag.

Stony will be in Ann Arbor this semester only, while he's back in Michigan to visit his family. Although he keeps no regular schedule, he can most likely be seen on Wednesdays or Thursdays in front of the Graduate Library. There are also plans for a television show on Ann Arbor Channel 9 and 10 entitled "Stony Speaks."

Although Preacher Mike refused to comment directly on his competition, he did give his advice on how to spot a bad soapbox speaker, "Some are too mean," he said. "Or just plain silly."

Well Hello Dali

Of my many brushes with the famous and important, there is one event that sticks out in my mind. That was the day I met the Dali Lama in Ann Arbor, Michigan. The year was 1993. Jewel Heart was the name of the Buddhist organization that brought the Dali Lama to Michigan. The Dali Lama was making some of his first visits to the USA and the whole of Michigan was abuzz with his presence. It only took him how many reincarnations to make it to Tree Town USA? And the tickets for the man who eschews material wealth were sky high. Since 1955 the Tibetans had lost their sovereignty to Mao's "People's Army." In 1959 the Dali Lama was exiled to India. Stateless, homeless, but nevertheless spreading the love on a globe-trotting carpet of hospitality as a result of his enormous popularity, which I guess had built up over several reincarnations. Being the mortal I was, I resigned myself to perhaps getting a glimpse of him passing in between buildings.

Packing my trusty camcorder, I hoped just for a glimpse in the lenses that I could parlay into a segment of my public cable access TV show "Stoney Speaks." Like a gunslinger of the old west I keep practicing pointing my camera, clicking "record." If even a glint of the enlightened fog starts rolling my way I will be ready. I wait, and wait. First comes Richard Gere, followed shortly after by Allen Ginsberg. Finally the long wait is over and the Dali Lama comes floating out of Hill Auditorium on a cloud of awe and incense. The large throng of people waiting outside surges forward, then parts slowly like the tide retreating to the sea. That grin spreads quickly around his face. At this point he was a good 50 feet away,

and to my dismay he started to work the crowd with no particular intent to follow the celebrities that had come before him. He
looked awful happy considering his people's plight. Or was that a
cosmic smirk, a tattoo of folly he has earned? Like when you hear
a really good joke and it stays with you the next week.

He's now ambling along, making his way in zig-zag fashion in
my general direction. I fiddle nervously with my camera, careful
to adjust the focus and set tape to speed. His deliberate, and plod-
ding path opens before him as he seems to be in no rush at all to
leave the spring sunshine. Before I know it, the Dali Lama is a few
feet away. If his trajectory continues we will have a soft collision
sometime soon. I look down to tweak the viewfinder, and check
the battery levels one more time. I lift my camera up only to find
him very fuzzy and off kilter. Lo and behold he is right in front of
me. I mean face to face. Close enough to see that he must have
been flossing for thousands of years, and his smile washing over
me like a warm west wind. I quickly make the spiritually correct
decision to lower my camcorder. I put my media gun back in its
holster, so to speak, and have no choice but to talk with the man
himself.

By the time the million stars in his eyes are shining at me, I
manage to utter a hushed, but sincere, "Peace To You."

The Dali Lama cocks his head slightly, moves closer, and stares
intently "What?"

After gargling my words for a second, I manage to repeat my
greeting.

He throws his head back and gives out a breezy laugh. "Peace to
you too," he says as he shakes my hand steadily. For just a moment I
was hurtled through centuries of Eastern enlightenment. The twin-
kle in his eyes gave way to a slight exhale that passed over me like a
refreshing breeze. His manner was very subtle, like the cooling mist
at an ocean's edge that holds off the heat of the day. He squeezed
my hand one more time, before moving on to the next person.

I never did turn my camcorder on. Yet the event is forever on pause in my memory. Many years later I picked up a Buddhist monk in my SF taxi and recounted the story I tell here. He told me that this Dali Lama had the uncanny sense to know who needed a touch, or look in the eye. Somehow he ferreted out my sorrow, tuned in his sad-o-meter at the imminent passing of my mother, Betty.

How did he know that I needed the soothing wind that wafts off the ocean of love to calm my stormy soul? At that very moment in the universe he was looking at me! I am almost sure I would never say that I don't believe in that great and wondrous unknown. For that is only known to those who know. The Dali Lama once said, "Remember one thing, not getting what you want is sometimes a wonderful stroke of luck." Indeed, today I was lucky, and it didn't cost me a dime.

Religious Characters

This story can't be told without giving a nod to all the religious characters who have vied for the same physical/spiritual spot, on a sunny day, in the struggle for young and impressionable minds. As I traveled around to campuses, there was always a local religious book thumper who was told by God to take the best speaking spot on campus, all week long, for as many years as possible. Who is writing these rules? That is par for the course until Stoney shows up with a dream on his lips that God had trusted him with as well. In my dream, my marching orders were clear: to chase down, confront, and discredit the hypocrites who speak of a vindictive and revengeful God. One has to know a little about the Bible, and a lot about world history, to even stand a chance against the twisted and rhetorically back-flipped religious worldview. From my angle, looking at the circle we all share, I'd say all the prayers go to the same place, like merging onto a freeway of love light. We are all standing in a circle, seeing the truth in the middle, from a different angle. Not being afraid to be condemned to hell takes some getting used to. That is the God-grease drone they slither on when they are desperate. Some Bible thumpers have even sent me hate mail that I'm sure even Jesus sent back just two stamps short of karma payback for the chump who's wasting a death threat on a unemployed street performer.

I would never be foolish enough to say I don't "believe," as that in itself is an admission of belief in something.

One day in the '90s I was going to hear and "chat" with Bible wonder boy "Cliff" on the SFSU plaza. The SF State plaza was filled for hours with our animated back and forth tackling of religions

STONEY SPEAKS

BIZARRE LOVE LETTER FROM A
WEAK MINDED INDIVIDUAL.

Stoney

you need to get your _filthy_ mind out of the gutter of _anti god_
socialist thought. You are simply a puppet of evil. You are a
pawn of the devil and will be eternal fuel in the flames of hell
as the demons mock and laugh at your miserbale life. But the
simple fact is your character is so evil and selfish you will
find the crack and pop of gods wrath in hell is exactly what you
deserve. All of hell rejoices each day you exist and god and the
angels are vexed with your existence. Yet the blood of christ
continues to call for your wicked soul as you trample, mock, and
hate the one who seeks your pardon. Stoney you will get your due
and your mounting guilt grows each moment you resist his call. I
know you continue in your mocking way and evil agenda in
attempting to quiet the shame you feel.Today God requires you to
give up your present selfish pursuits of the gratification of
your sensibilities at Gods expense

J. 5.5 Brother John

the right not to believe in anothers religion is just as
important as the the right to explore your own relationship
with the unknown. I only wish Brother John would have kept his
not so veiled death threats in his church in Georgia....where
they belong. Peace....Stoney

Hate Letter Via Bible Guy

**Stoney and Bible guy debate on Red Square,
University of Washington, Seattle**

greatest questions. I won, when one of his disciples threw lemon-
ade in my face. Cliff stood silent, stoic, he gave his blessing. The
next day the SFSU school newspaper, in their letters to the editor
section, had me branded as a blasphemer. As I was reading the
paper in front of the Student Union, the Black Muslim Student
Union was having its rally on the free speech spot to deliver a verbal death against Salmon Rushdie. Excuse me? I could have sworn
that just last week, death threats were not included in this Free
Speech game we play? This downgrade in speech politics would
take some adjusting to on my part. I live by the motto *don't let your
mouth write checks your butt can't cash.*

Oh oh ... I looked down at the newspaper, and up at the words
being spoken, up and back, up and back. I decided right there
and then to make an adjustment. The small but mighty porcu-
pine has razor quills that can stick and kill. It was duly noted, I
must avoid backing into the prickly monotheist doctrines that are,
like the oil companies, of the spirit world. Reliable pumping of
cheap words, 'til there's a spill of lies so big it wipes out the moral
compass. There is nothing in the world besides talking about religion or sex that gets a crowd all worked up. On any given day, I'd
choose one or the other to rattle the can. By "worked up" I mean
get a few folks engaged in thought, ready to dialogue, and anxious
to rumble for their cause.

I am proud to say that I have never had a physical fight break
out at or near my shows. I would intercede long before it was
headed that way. We are not talking about cops or provocateurs
here. Having said that, there is nothing wrong with a heated discussion about the role of religion, government, and humankind,
and whatever else, out in the open air. There you can raise your
voice, tweak your timbre, and ramp up your emotive state, without
the word police hauling you off for legal examination. For that is
the ultimate test of Democracy. Are your words so dangerous, that
you must be removed physically from the space to ensure "peace"?

A Typical Day

Typical day in the life of Stoney? ... There is none, and when it becomes routine is when the pitbulls jump the fence and sneak up on you. The one day in the week when I can put on my costume and pretend to create the truth that I wish was – becomes the Sunday in my free speech worship week. To weave-wave a magic wand that can last more than an hour. Be the performer I might see on TV, what a concept, eh? A dream as old as the sun, here's the best part, it's free, and you can do it yourself! It sure beats the alternative, whatever that may be.

What is famous? Everybody does something unique and worthy, so famous is a relative term isn't it? Is it *all* about the money? As for myself, like most people, I mistakenly associate famous with wealthy. Maybe I secretly envy grey suits and red ties that pull down a cool slice of the pie without suffering the scrutiny of the IRS. But talent, that's another ball of wax. You know it when you see it, if you have trained your eye to see, that is. If not, your eye trains you to "see" the shell of poseur wealth. Everybody's 15 minutes of fame has been woven into a quilt of egos and great technical prowess nowadays, and can give that 15 digital minutes a run at years and years. That is par for the course. Alas, there is more than meets the eye. What goes on when the camera is not on ... is more important than a reality-based TV show based on your life. Or goddess forbid, we are doomed to volunteering for Big Brother. This is the long way of saying that performing without the intent of recording or documenting the event is more fun than the opposite. Now ... who has a camera, and operator I can borrow?

Photo: Gary Ivanek

Masks on Stoney

Street Performers, People, and Places

(What Memories Are Made Of)

Reverend Chumly ... University of Oregon courtyard, late seventies. Clown who performed the amazing Peruvian mating dance with two walnuts.

Roar ... Muscle bound man who upon request would – rrrrrrr-roar – really loud!

Happy Happy Man ... Never quite got his message besides "Be Happy."

The Human Jukebox ... The now-deceased Grimes! If you gave him a quarter, he'd play two notes and shut his flap. If you gave him a dollar, he'd play that wacky clarinet for a whole song.

Jim Page ... Satirical/protest/guitar player in the courtyard of the University of Oregon in the '70s. To this day, a legend in Seattle.

Zoo Zoo the Clown ... An expatriate from San Francisco who taught me to juggle in Amsterdam, whereabouts unknown.

Jango Edwards ... A Michigan native and one of the most famous clowns in the Netherlands, perhaps the world. I performed with my own troupe in his Festival of Fools.

Moonman ... Sold acres of the moon for $1.00. Berkeley, USA, early '70s. Whereabouts unknown.

Rick Starr ... Neo legendary Frank Sinatra wannabe, but could not sing. He looked like his life began and ended in 1944. Our duets on "Chicago" were memorable. Whereabouts unknown.

The Hate Man ... If you hated him, it was the right thing to do. OC = Original Crazies. Still resides in People's Park, Berkeley, CA.

Hate Boy ... Understudy of the above, and just as hateful.

Polka Dot Guy ... "William," who can still be seen at UCB, with a bucket over his head, or some crazy found object invention, dispensing crazy wisdom to the unsuspecting. He is seen in my film "An American in America" (viewable on YouTube).

Wayne Doba ... Danced the tap like no one else I've seen. Dressed to the nines, '40s style, rubber faced. As a duo, we entertained the King Tut exhibit crowds in front of the old De Young museum, in Golden Gate Park. See him in the film "Scarface!"

Swami X ... Last seen on YouTube 2009, getting an award of commemoration by the LA Mayor. The Mayor remarks, "I am a UCLA grad, and he would be there on Bruin walk every day of the week." (Remarks were quite similar to San Francisco Supervisor Sandoval's take on memories regarding me.)

The Silver Lady ... Louisa, a sleek and tireless robot who had a special spot in front of the Ferry Building in SF. Underneath the shiny suit is actually a stunning beauty and brilliant scientist now working at NASA.

Dave Lippmann ... One of the great musical satirists of our day. Sings in "An American in America." He sings, "I Hate Walmart." Will never sell at said venue.

San Francisco Mime Troupe ... The big Kahunas of "perform in the parks for free" every summer. I first saw SFMT at the WOW hall in Eugene, Oregon. Their adaptation of Dario Fo's "We Can't Pay, We Won't Pay" left me teary-eyed, open-hearted, and choked up. I was not alone in the kitchen cooking up humor and politics for working-class America. They must be good, for they are original inductees into the SATIRE HALL OF FAME.

Dr. Hot and his Thermal Medicine Show ... They played with me at the old Boarding house, Other Café, and various venues in San Francisco. I eventually followed them to Amsterdam, where I lived in Dr. Hot's van for a cold winter next to the Prinsengracht Canal. Last seen at the Oregon Country Fair in 2012.

Preacher Eddie ... "Stoney is going to Hell."

Preacher Glenn ... "Stoney is going to Hell."

Sister Cindy and Brother Jed ... "Stoney is going to Hell."

Cliff the Evangelist ... "Stoney is going to Hell!"

Holy Hubert ... Old-time religious street preacher in the '70s. "Stoney is going to hell, but not before I tell you how mad I am at you and the whole damned world of homosexuals, perverts and communists." Drew the largest crowds I had ever seen for a Bible guy.

Eskimo ... Street band in Berkeley, California that recorded a "StoneySpeaks TV" theme song with the classic lyrics – "When Stoney speaks to me, I cannot leave the room, to eat or pee." Whereabouts unknown.

Steve Lightfoot ... "Stephen King and *Time* magazine killed John Lennon!" Conspiracy theorist. Had the money and gumption to drive around in a van with a speaker on top exclaiming his bizarre theories.

Cosmic Lady ... Ex-wife of Diamond Dave. Rainbow woman of deep thoughts, peaceful vibes, and intergalactic love energy.

Amazing tap dancer ... A 4x4 piece of plywood, sweat, dazzling feet, and tourist coins, San Francisco, California.

Jimi Hendrix impersonator ... "Excuse me while I pass the hat." Streets of San Francisco, California.

James Brown impersonator ... Could not sing, but had the spin move. San Francisco, California.

Charley Barnett ... Deceased. Famed NYC street performer. Would draw immense crowds to his Washington Square park shows. Featured in the film "Taxi" (the Mr. T version).

The Puppet Man ... Deceased. Old man with funny puppets and hearty laugh at San Francisco State University. Made me laugh.

Scott the piano player ... Gershwin and Pop in the sun, UCB.

Dave Temple ... Joshua. "World will end in 88 days." When the world did not end, he would start the doomsday clock again. What a beautiful scam.

Chris ... The "get off your cell phone" guy, annoy artist, semiretired, UCB.

Judi Foster ... Founder of East Bay Food Not Bombs. She was a force of nature and humanity. Your heart swelled, and you tried to be your best around her.

Ralph ... the guy with no hands playing blues on a slide guitar. San Francisco, California.

Plaza Rats ... Those who hang at the plaza, waiting for something to happen.

Ed Weber ... Librarian, roommate, and guardian of the Labadie Collection at University of Michigan.

John "JD" Dalton ... Studio tech at Berkeley Community Media. A paraplegic who despite physical limitations produced a bevy of excellent "StoneySpeaks TV" episodes. Went on to found the legendary punk band The Angry Amputees.

Jonathon Winters ... The king of improv! My main guru of the HA.

Mike the Preacher ... At University of Michigan Diag. Epic verbal/spiritual battles of biblical proportions 1990s. ("Stoney is going to hell.")

Chinese Clowns ... Jane and her Mom. Funny, and for real.

John Fizer ...   the folk singer in "An American in America," Homeless to this day, but does hands down the best version of "Mr. Bojangles" I've ever heard. See him on YouTube.

Noam Chomsky ... Passes by my spot, declines to speak, as he is on his way to a class a UC Berkeley. Respectful applause from audience and awe from me.

Wesley Snipes ... Stops by my spot. Flanked by two humongous bodyguards as he takes a break from filming "The Fan" in San Francisco.

Every Chancellor ... That passed by my spot and pretended not to see me.

The Trees ... By the Memorial stadium ripped from the roots to make way for a football team that never wins due to the "OPPENHEIMER CURSE." (You made the bomb, now you lose the big game forever.) UC Berkeley.

Tiny Patton ... Cigar-chomping, bike-riding character, all around expert on nothing, but never afraid to let you know how much you never knew about the history of Romeo, Michigan until he happened by.

Romeo Basketball, Baseball and Beyond ... Three generations of Cushinberrys, Pistol Pete Dalton, Don Throops home plate in my backyard, and Jacobs '62 Dodge Dart fueled by pizza on the back roads of post-game critiques.

Bob Sparks ... Berkeley activist and People's Park devotee. I learned a lot about facing the "Beast on the Hill" and fighting the good fight from him. He left us too soon, but we'll keep on Bob, we promise.

Stupid ... Senior Communist Jokester in Eugene, Oregon. In the late 1970s. Printed and sold an array of wacky left-wing material. His peace plan? "Mandatory Cannibalism. You kill it, you eat it!"

Don, **"The Red Ribbon Man"** ... During the long struggle to end Apartheid in South Africa, Don would be the guy you got a red ribbon of solidarity from to pin on your lapel. (And you better have it on next time he sees you!)

Bishop Joey ... He took over April Fool's Day in San Francisco, California, and made it Saint Stupid's Day. He, his wife Janet, and a cast of a thousand clowns have been parading through the City by the Bay for over 35 years. Free and open to the public as always.

Barney "Sweetgrass" ... My Native American drum instructor at SFSU who would scowl at my white-guy lack of rhythm and remark occasionally, "You sound like a herd of buffalo stampeding over the skin."

The Bubble Lady Julia Vinograd ... "Breakfast in Berkeley, brown hash, and hash browns."

Paul Krassner ... Author, rabble rouser, and mentor to me. Founding member of the Yippies and Satire Hall of Fame.

Farley ... Director of "Citizen," poet, friend, and the one who first told me of the "street performer's curse." ("When you start that low, it's tough to get much higher.") I have him to thank for my trip to Amsterdam.

Skidway Hilton ... A real and mythical place "up north." Where the Rifle River runs clean, down a dirt road, and close to my heart.

Leroy Moore ... Frequent guest on "StoneySpeaks TV," and the founder of KRIP HOP NATION. Leroy opened my eyes to the artistry of people using Hip Hop to tell their story from the perspective of the "physically challenged."

Casa Dominick's Wall ... There have been days on the Diag when getting hassled by DPS, or arguing with a Military Science major is just too much. That's when I retreat to the veranda of "Dom's" with a cool flask of Sangria. The people's history of Ann Arbor is hanging just above my head. There's the fifty-year-old poster of the first Ann Arbor Film Festival, just down from a faded photo of SDS unknowns plotting peace over a wooden table. To survive history in this town, you have to be on a wall.

Photo by Helen Holt

The Space Lady

Perhaps the most recognizable street musician in San Francisco, California from the 1970s to the 2000s.

The World Is Ending – Dave Temple

William the Polka Dot Man

Sometimes
The Rage Bubbles Up

Sometimes, I just feel so frustrated with life. Like trying to put a fire out with a squirt gun. No matter what I do, the rage seeps to the surface like oil on Jed's farm. Yes, there is something wrong with me, just like everybody. I should seek help, and I will. Until then I have my days on the Plaza, where I can blow off some steam. For that I give praise to my real-time circumstances. I could be worse.

Stoney finally finishes college after 19 years

Stoney's College Yearbook

Stoney and friend Lauren Hatvany at SFSU

"I Survived SFSU" graduate

Cops Chase Stoney At University Of Oregon Or Hands Up! (1992)

♦♦♦♦

O n this trip I met, and talked to, Bill Clinton. This was on the campaign trail of 1992, and I was in full Uncle Sam costume. I worked my way to the front of the crowd, as always, with my "CLOWN VIP" pass. Clinton gave a rousing, and almost believable, send-up of the Democratic talking points of the time. He was a brilliant Southern expostulator, endowed with the arrogance of a power-drunk dogcatcher. And, yes, I voted for him. Given the alternatives, was there really a choice? I'm trying to be fair and balanced. Props to Will Rogers, who said, "I am not a member of any organized political party. I am a Democrat."

Clinton was the sort of politician who might be crooked in a good way, for your side if you knew how to bet and win. On that day, I had cornered Clinton and asked him about one of his rivals, Ross Perot. "I tell you," Clinton growled, as he wagged his yet-to-be-Lewinsky-famed finger, "we'll just see who'll be the cat to catch in the next three months. Perot will not be a factor in this race!" Luckily for Clinton, and some would say for our country, Perot WAS a factor. By sucking up 20% of the vote in that election, Perot divided the GOP into the Dumb and Dumber camps.

Was it better for us that Clinton won? I would argue that NAFTA was a big business scamola, no matter which candidate won. The pawn played his role, and even helped to usher in Bush 2.0. The Mighty Ross Perot finally backed down, claiming the Bush Machine was out to destroy his family and steal the election. DUH. That's something I could have told him, "plain and simple," was going to happen. The wackiest thing I ever heard from Ross Perot was his idea that the deficit was so big, if you took all of the richest people's money and threw it at the debt, it would not solve the problem. Well, he still has his $3 billion, and we still have nothing. Now that's wacky.

The picture on the following page was taken just after the police have retreated. The students and onlookers formed a protective cordon around me to prevent the police from seizing me. With the help of some true believers and a bit of Irish luck, I was swimmimg in Free Speech bliss.

WE resisted that day. I can still see the cops' hands thrusting through the crowd. Their weak little hands twitched like falling leaves. All of their weapons, and the State, could not sew my lips together. For a moment, we stood our ground, and won. That is my Kung Fu … and it was strong.

Cops chase Stoney at Oregon State University – mellow! I can still see Barney Fife and his partner running across the freshly mowed lawn with handcuffs in their hands. The crowd was just getting into the diatribe, the laughs were flowing, and then all hell broke loose. Whatever happened that day to the customary "what the hek is going on here" intro? These two cops were bounding down on me like a brake-broken dump truck. In basketball if you hold very still, and get bowled over, it's an offensive foul. On this day the legal refs calling the shots were leaning toward injustice.

Oregon Daily

THURSDAY, MAY 21, 1992   **EUGENE, OREGON**

Stoney Burke speaks to a crowd of students on the lawn in front of Condon Hall Wednesday afternoon. The students circled Burke to keep OPS and EPD officers from serving him with a letter of trespass.

San Francisco street performer Stoney Burke passes out postcards of himself to students Thursday at the Memorial Union Building at Oregon State University.

Police tell OSU 'performer' to mellow

By Michael Schmieman

"An impromptu show" by a San Francisco street performer caused some tense moments Thursday for two Oregon State University security officers.

The incident started at about 12:36 p.m. when Memorial Union officials called campus security to complain about a man shouting profanities in the Quad.

The subject of the complaint was a green-haired, San Francisco native named Stoney Burke.

By the time the officers arrived, a crowd of about 30 people had gathered around Burke, who was in the midst of what he later called "a diatribe against the monolithic system of power and money."

Lt. Phil Mohr of the state police said the officers never intended to arrest Burke, only ask him to "mellow out a little."

However, Burke had worked himself into a frenzy, Mohr said, prompting the officers to handcuff him before taking him inside the Memorial Union to discuss the situation further.

At this point, the crowd began "bumping and grabbing" at the officers, who called for assistance, as the crowd followed them into the building, Mohr said.

Seven uniformed officers from the Corvallis Police Department and an undisclosed number of state police units responded to the call.

Once inside, Burke was very cooperative, Mohr said. "He said he was a street performer from San Francisco. I told him it was OK to express his feelings as long as he didn't try to incite the crowd."

Burke agreed to take his "show" back outside and "mellow out," Mohr said. "He did exactly what he said he would."

In a later interview, Burke said he has been touring college campuses for years, advocating free speech and railing against inequalities in the system.

He said he has been arrested about 20 times.

His expenses are met, in part, by donations he solicits from the crowds he generates when he starts to "perform."

Although Burke declined to say how much money he collected Thursday, he called it a "good" day.

"When you don't collect any money AND get arrested, that's a bad day," he said.

Office of the President-elect
and Vice President-elect

January 12, 1993

Stoney Burke
519 Castro, #29
San Francisco, CA 94114-2577

Dear Stoney:

Thank you for sending me the video cassette. I have received many thoughtful gifts
and suggestions from people all across America. I appreciate your enthusiasm and
support. Thanks.

Sincerely,

Bill Clinton

Bill Clinton

BC/gen

Letter To Stoney From President Clinton

A Thank You From Bill Clinton

As well he should have. "Stoney Does Houston" was nothing less than a cult classic, pre-YouTube phenomenon. The best guerilla, shoot-from-the-hip reporting in the history of journalism.

Don't take it from me; see it for yourself on YouTube. I met the director, Bob Hercules, while I was performing on the Diag, at University of Michigan. Since the early '80s, we have collaborated on projects that, in my opinion, are MORE than just memorable. Hey, this is my book, and I'm doing the remembering!

Stoney Does Houston

by John Carlos Cantú

[1992, Directed by Bob Hercules. Cast: Stoney Burke and more Republicans than you can shake a fist at. Ann Arbor Community Access Channel 9. 15 mins.]

D ig him or not, Stoney Burke – Ann Arbor's resident soapbox philosopher – gets the job done.

Who else would venture into the bosom of the Grand Old Party's heartland to seek what truth lay in the heart of the then Bush administration? Burke's director, Bob Hercules, does a remarkably thorough job of covering everyone who was anyone at the 1992 Republican National Convention held at the Astrodome on August 17–20, 1992. The Republican Party of that year is quickly examined in decisive strokes from the top to bottom within the limited resources of public access television.

Likewise, Burke's "take no prisoners" approach to his quarry on the convention floor creates some fabulous Cinéma vérité. Bruce Willis' smirk has been nabbed intact; Robert Novak pontificates with worldly wisdom; Pat Robertson pontificates with otherworldly wisdom; and Alfonse D'Amato proves himself to be the reigning jerk of American politics.

The wonder of "Stoney Does Houston" is just that. How did he do Houston? On a couple of occasions Burke identifies himself as a PBS reporter (at least now we know why Congress is so busily hammering public broadcasting). But far more important: how did he snare the credentials to pull off this scam? It's too good to be true.

On a more mundane level, Burke does what any decent

reporter is supposed to do: Ask the hard questions. In fact, Burke does such a good job of asking these questions, he highlights much of current media's inability to do its job. For disclaimers about journalistic legitimacy aside, there are very few journalists – and particularly very few television reporters – who are willing to bite off the serious issues of the day.

Stoney does so with an "in-your-face" vengeance.

Given that the atmosphere of any political gathering is surreal,"Stoney Does Houston" has a definite surreal ambiance.

Stoney doing Houston

Stoney at Republican Convention Houston, TX, 1992

Hypocrisy In A Box

You've probably asked yourself by now: How in the hek does he make any money at this vocation? If a good day of rabble-rousing might lead to an arrest, and a great day might lead to free coffee, how does he make a living? I've asked myself that very question many times, and I've rarely given the same answer. Well, I have to work, like everybody else. Most of the time, I've worked at jobs which enable me to continue my life as a Free Speecher.

I've worked every odd, lowdown, sweat-in-the-sun or drive-round-and-round job to keep it going. Given enough time and will-power, I could usually find the job that would be a means to that end. For me, any potential job had to include the following criterion: Can I get off Tuesday at noon, so I can go and rant on the quad like I don't have a job? Surely one day a week to be authentically ME can't be too much to ask of an employer? It's got to be freedom first, and money second. Granted, it is a thin line I tread. I dance madly as poverty pursues me. Rarely, if ever, have I been able to tell the Boss what I really did in my spare time.

I'm a proud member of the "Workers Against Work Union." We're united in our belief that work is what we do for others, and love is what we do for each other. Work is necessary, however, and there's no way around doing the best I can at whatever I'm doing. I've been a janitor, cemetery worker, basketball referee, pickle factory slave, recreation leader, daycare worker, gardener, actor, forest service fireman, short order cook, Christmas tree killer, phone solicitor, bodyguard to the stars, and taxi driver. The ones I have omitted are so far under the radar, they are best left unmentioned.

One such attempt to fund my Free Speech brought me to the syringed gates of the most corrupt scam in the USA: The Health Industry. The sea of corruption wherein fluids are withdrawn and money is exchanged. Millions of human lives are kept floating in the ethers, powered by prescription drugs, and HMOs engorged on triplicate billing.

Of the top ten jobs I wish I'd never taken, there's one in particular that crashed head on into my personal belief system. The job was at a medical diagnostic company, and I have omitted their name to protect the guilty. In 1996, I returned to my beloved SF Bay Area seeking a new leaf to be turned. As I was nearly broke, and it promised Tuesdays off, I had no choice but to take the job as driver/courier. This way I could do my Stoney thing at UCB. Just what I was looking for?

For starters, I had to wear a sewage-green uniform with large, red lettering on the shirt and hat. I would pick up all kinds of fluids: blood, urine, body tissues, jars of fecal matter, and ferry them to various hospitals and clinics on my route. We were instructed never to allow these fecal jars to thaw, as they had been known to explode under the right conditions. We called these jars "Dung-Bombs."

Anything that could be put in a vial, scanned, and diagnosed was left in the fridge for me, the medical courier guy. I picked 'em up, and shipped 'em out. The weapons I was issued to protect myself from these bags of contagion were rubber gloves, dry ice containers, and a clipboard. There was a mountain of paperwork to occupy my spare moments. All of this for $8.00 per hour and no benefits. My boss took all of this pee very seriously. And they wonder why good people turn to crime.

Quickly, I became adept at donning my rubber gloves and handling all sorts of medical specimens. Laboring all day under the constant threat of a "Fecal Strafing" was far better than the daily attempt at happy talk with my boot-licking boss. What really bothered me, though, was the incredible volume of urine samples we picked up for drug screening. At this point I freely admit that, not unlike a former President, I've only inhaled once in my life. I've just never exhaled. This detour to the corporate world would put me on a collision course with my employment destiny.

Every day, I would pick up 40 to 50 vials of urine. Drug screens. These plastic vials were packed in cardboard boxes, and each box represented another person who was forced to drain their precious fluids in the presence of a trained medical technician. The next link in the screw-the-worker chain was me, the courier. I picked up these specimens and made my way back to our office, my truck loaded to the gills with the futures of workers all over the country. This job was so pointless, corrupt, and boring that I was forced to self-medicate so I wouldn't self-harm. Whether or not someone was promoted, fired, or arrested depended on my prompt attention to the task at hand. How many people could rightly have said that their test results were invalid because their specimen was delivered by a stoner?

During the long drive back to Oakland, the freeway creepy creeps would engulf my mind, and work their way into my guilty conscience. Each bump would jostle another utterance from the vials in the back. As I braked hard for a curve, their voices rose. The Incarcerated Urine shouted, "HYPOCRITE." When I stopped at a traffic light, the pee yelled, "WHO ARE YOU TO HELP THE FASCISTS PUT ME OUT ON THE STREET?"

Scrooge-like, I'd shake off the voices by telling myself it was just fatigue, or that a bad burrito had soured my stomach. Night after night, on the drive home, I'd imagine the urine morphing and crystallizing into the faces of the very people whose pee I had made off with. Was that just a wisp of fog, or was it the drug-tested pizza delivery girl staring at me with spicy pepperoni eyes?

Is that strange clicking noise my car's CV joint, or have the boxes become piranhas, opening and closing their lids to expose their angry teeth? In my mind's eye, they pursued me down an Amazon of urine.

You see, what was actually in each box was not just a hygienically obtained specimen, but a real person, forced humiliatingly to squat over a stool with their pants down. They were begging me to pull over and dump them out by the side of the road. All of the bumps and squeaks had merged into a chorus of FREE THE PEE!

The weight of my hypocrisy danced like a hundred bowling balls on my forever-damned soul. Here I was, making the money for my own "Medication" by delivering drug screens to the Feds in their war on the poor. I'm sure Bernie Madoff never made tinkle in a cup with a nurse waiting outside the door. If he had, would it have sounded anything like the tinkle-tinkle of his Ponzi scheme gone amok?

So, I keep my eyes on the road. Surely, if I were to stop, the vials would leap out the window and disappear amongst the farm workers in the fields, undocumented pee without the proper papers. Why, the whole shipment might be lost.

Once home, after the guilt had built up in the bladder of my conscience, I'd develop elaborate rescue scenarios to relieve my moral discomfort. One such fantasy placed me in a mock barn, inside which all specimens would be exchanged for stolen toilet water from Mormon temples. After these altered samples were analyzed, there would be millions of negative results, whereby evil labs would lose millions of dollars in revenue and go out of business. I'd be laid off, and thus released from my duties as diagnostic night porter.

One night after picking up my car, I took off and neatly folded my uniform. With my clipboard, rubber gloves, and one stray urine sample, I left the following note: "I've just tested positive for freedom. See ya later!" Somewhere in a dusty culvert north of San

Francisco, there is a wet patch of soil, escaped urine that was freed by my hand. It felt like "LIBERPEE." To this day I am a dues paying member of the ULF – the Urine Liberation Front.

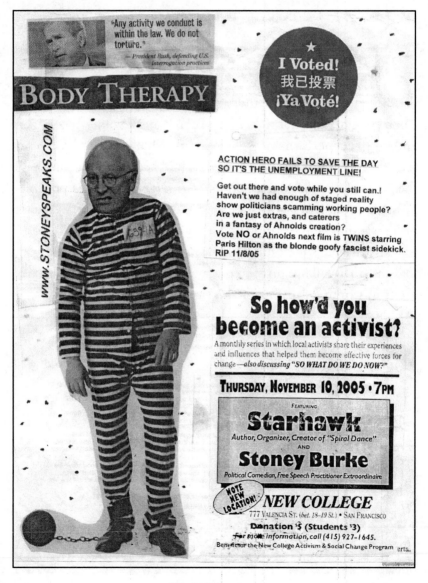

Dick Cheney

Taxi

Driving taxi is like life. You never know who you're going to pick up, and you never know where you're going, but you sure as hek hope there's some money waiting at the end. Then you start another ride. In between being a Public Access icon and my street performances, I have to do what everyone else in my lofty position must do – get a second job, keep working, and pull the casino lever marked *LUCK and CHANCE* as often as possible. "Work is a four-letter word," I would joke to my customers. "Please don't use that kind of language in my cab!"

Taxi driving suited me. Once you strap yourself into the seat, log on to Dispatch, and say your prayers to St. Christopher, you are truly working for yourself. So you'd better be good.

Stoney Drives Taxi

They say to be a good taxi driver, you have to get along with the whole world, but only for 20 minutes at a time. The ride, or life for that matter, won't last forever. Lean back and make the most of the ride you've got left.

Seven reasons why taxi driving is like life:

1. You never know who's going to flag you down, hop in your life, and take you for a ride.

2. If you have the money, someone will take you almost anywhere.

3. It's a lot easier to tell your life story to a stranger than your best friend.

4. Saying "Yes, Sir. No, Ma'am," and opening a door or two doesn't cost you a dime, and it usually gets you a return of respect and understanding.

5. If your wheels aren't turning, you're not making money. Get your life in gear and get a roll going.

6. The money on the meter at work, or in your cab, can never quite catch up with the bills in your life.

7. It's best to know where you're going before you move your car or life. At least use a map, and if you are heading into the Valley of Doom, ask directions for an alternate route.

What Is A Rabble Rouser?

No, it's not a standup comic who points out the quirks of his/her millionaire friends, nor is it the incessantly whining noted politician who benefits from the system of graft. Rousing the rabble is no easy chore and takes the commitment of someone who expects no reward besides the uplifting of the rabble's consciousness to some sort of acknowledgement of the crimes at hand. Soundly roused, maybe get out the vote or stop a war.

Jim, Tom, Cabin

GIs tell of orders to get rough

Prince Harry regrets attending party dressed as a Nazi soldier

U.S. ends search for WMDs

WHO ARE WE NOW? Can anyone tell me which way this ship of fools is headed to next? Here we have a full-blown war, historic debt and job loss figures, international natural disasters like the Tsunami ... in light of all that, our Bush-O-Rama is using his political capital gains to lavish upon himself a $40 million back-slapping get together on 1/20/05 with the same posse who brought you the WAR. Why did the Democrats lose? Kerry never came out against the WAR!!! No WMD'S? Torture of prisoners? Illegal detentions? Jack boot patriot act? None of these issues were on the agenda. Killing people who you don't know from 20,000 feet with an errant bomb is more moral than two gay people getting married on a sunny day in June? I really don't get it sometimes. These are dark days, when all those that truly believe in truth and freedom with be tested. PEACE ... Stop the WAR!!

FREE

Berkeley Daily Planet

Hungry for power

Mock council votes to leave Union, build Hearst statue and re-create Telegraph

BY LURENE HELZER
DAILY PLANET STAFF

In a shameless display of naked and self-serving power, the Berkeley Mock City Council tripped, buffooned and lampooned its way through whatever could pass as "city business" Tuesday evening.

Take the resolution for free-drug, er, drug free zones in the city, addressed during the second council session.

"I realize I'm drunk ... on power," said Councilmember Salmanilla, played by Karen Ripley. "But everyone knows drugs are not free there."

Councilmember Gruve, more commonly known to friends and family as Hali Hammer, said she could solve the whole sign controversy if the city manager (Kurt Reinhardt) could just "front me a couple hundred

dollars." He did.

As Councilmember Stoney - played by Stoney Burke - took off his shirt, he announced that after the meeting he was heading back to El Cerrito where the nudity laws were "liberal" and "he could get a jury trial." During the first session of the evening, he removed his shirt in the midst of a gender debate, to demonstrate how he - the character, mind you - had once been a woman.

That same session resulted in the city's declaration of independence from the United States, an increase in the minimum wage to $175 per hour and the approval of a statue honoring Patty "Tanya" Hearst's exploits as a bank robber.

The Hearst debate drew some of the heartiest laughter

PHOTOS BY ROB CUNNINGHAM/
DAILY PLANET STAFF

Top, Councilmember Stoney (played by Stoney Burke) takes off his shirt during the Mock City Council meeting. Above, individuals with grievances could ask the council for an apology.

See MOCK/Page 8

Mock City Council

The SF Bay is home to many mad geniuses and George Coates is one of them. By that I mean, he's a genius at getting the wrong people mad at him for mostly the right reasons. The Mock City Council was one of those events that happens only a couple times, before the real city council says, "Hey, you are making fun of ALL the politicians, that's not funny." I was fortunate to travel with George Coates in his production of "RareArea" to Europe and later I pinched myself as I stood on the stage at UC Berkeley's Zellerbach auditorium.

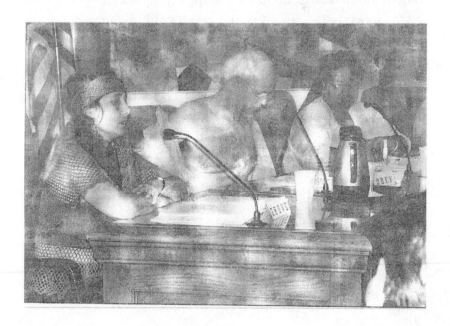

The Beast on the Hill

Every home, hamlet and neighborhood since who knows when, has to deal with an ogre of an institution that drains the fluid from the living and strikes a banker's pose on the way to the vault. In the case of Berkeley, it's the University of California at Berkeley. They are Masters of the Dark Sciences. A place where they invent the bomb, crush dissent, and feebly attempt to interpret history to suit themselves. On the other hand, its students were the first to cook LSD, set the national standard for the rights of the disabled, and gave birth to the Free Speech Movement. At the University of Michigan the dark sciences have gorged on Drone warfare technology. When I was in the Netherlands it was the monarchy vs. the squatters and so on. Every place I have spoken, in every state and country, there is a beast to be confronted. It's nothing personal, it's just in my nature to see it, say it, and try to do something about it. I'm certainly not the only one. For me it has always been important to separate the beast from the people who live in its shadow. Where is the beast in your neck of the woods?

Frat Boys Will Not Do Homework

Why it takes a comedian to tell the folks high on the hill the sun-burned truth is not that surprising. Al Franken is now a senator, and the biggest joke of all for a president (George W. Bush) has retired to where only the heat and horny toads have a sense of humor. If you actually put up a poster and offer work to the whiners who blame the Mexicans for the the white man's wall street crimes, you get fewer than a bushel of workers.

I for one grew up in a rural part of southeast Michigan, and for awhile did my share of back-breaking, sweat-draining work for what seemed even then a pittance. Without a doubt, a summer of haying a farmer's fields cured me of the desire to join the salt-of-the-earth-club. One day the farmer caught me and a buddy

sleeping under the shade of trees we were supposed to be prun-
ing. No, he didn't fire us. With a smirk and smile he sent us into
the barn to shovel knee-deep cow shit. We got the message, and
I was on to my next brilliant career move as a short order cook at
Big Boy.

The UFW has worked long and hard over the past fifty years
to organize the unwanted workers who till and harvest the fields.
When comedian Colbert hooked up with the UFW to start a TAKE
OUR JOBS campaign it was funny yet truth-telling. Few showed
up for the jobs, and the few that did took early retirement the
next day. Cheap labor is capitalism's dirty little secret. An army
of an underclass must subsidize the tier above all the way up the
pyramid.

I met Ceasar Chavez on the steps of Sproul Hall. His wrinkled
hands still gave a solid grip. If there were one big union, the farm
workers would be valued, not rousted like French Roma. Every
time I listen to multimillionaire Rush Limbaugh bluster on about
illegals, I wonder who picked his produce that day. I wonder who
cut his lawn. I doubt if it was Glenn Beck's frat boy army.

No ... they would all be down on the border holding hands
and hiring a mariachi band to play music they could not sing to
anyway.

Matrix Satire

My Matrix Reloaded

Aaaannnnd, the 8.3-second Oscar goes to … Stoney, in "Matrix Reloaded."

Whenever someone asks what I do and I reply, "Film actor" I know the next question will be, "And what films have you been in that I know of?" That is really a trick question, so sometimes I give a trick answer, rattling off the titles of the blockbusters I've been in. I just don't mention that I was a background actor in those films. If they seem genuinely interested, beyond the celebrity gossip and happy talk, I tell them that every film I've appeared in has been important to me, no matter how successful it was at the box office. But sometimes, I weave in my tale of the eight seconds I spent in "Matrix Reloaded," the second best-selling R-rated film of all time, second only to "The Passion of Christ."

I've been a member of the Screen Actors Guild since my role in Jonathan Parker's "Bartleby," and there are certain union-guaranteed perks given to Principal Actors. In addition to just being allowed on the film set, which is rewarding fun enough I suppose, a Principal Actor also gets treated like a human being. On the morning of my shoot at the Alameda Air Station, an unmarked white van came to my house in Oakland. I was loaded in and delivered to the set of "Matrix Reloaded." Upon arrival, I was ferried by golf cart to my trailer. MY trailer! Bike Carrier Driver, it said, on the door. That's ME! Then to Costume, which is the first stop in your journey of transformation, for clothes. Then to make-up, where you'd be surprised what magic they can do with a bald-headed, bespectacled white guy. In a swirl of friendly excitement, my metamorphosis is complete, and I'm rushed over to meet the Wachowski brothers. They approve.

On the way in the door, I met Aaliyah, the singer/actress who was replaced in this production after her tragic death. Through more security, and past the hangar door, we finally arrived at a large Blue Room. Inside, Laurence Fishburne is lying on top of a large, white vibrating box – a mock semi-truck. He's swatting at a lot of invisible flies, I think, when the tech guys start moving lights. For 20 minutes they adjusted these lights, giving the Wachowski brothers time to further look me over. One of them shoved a huge cowboy hat on my head, but I think I looked too comical in it, because they both laughed. They nixed the hat and spared me a lifetime of people asking me: "Hey Stoney, where's the cowboy hat?"

But, it's not all trailers and golf carts. My career as an extra in Hollywood films stretches from an unpaid extra in "Animal House" (FOOD FIGHT), to the halls of San Francisco City Hall in the Oscar-winning film "Milk." I did 60 takes in a row in the film "Zodiac," only to fail to make it into the final cut. That's showbiz!

Stoney Burke, truck driver, watches in disbelief as Trinity zooms off his semi on a motorcycle. From "Matrix Re loaded."

William Shatner's Hands

'm looking deep into my computer now: what appears to be my last chance at fame and fortune is nothing but robot software. Almost every day a new job comes in for me to either submit to or ignore. If only I could see the thousands of people who also submit their online portfolio, in hopes that their digitized image grabs a casting agent by the throat and says, "Hire this poor sucker!"

Just like the lottery, somebody has to win these roles, and as they say, you have to be in it to win it. Here's the next role for my fantasies to take hold of – it's the part of William Shatner's hands. Just his hands. But if so chosen they are your hands. Then by the looks of the contract, you'll be buying at least all the beans and rice for a year or so. How does one prepare to audition your damn hands?

Since I chew my cuticles at most auditions due to the stress, I figure my chance of being Captain Kirk's hands is about as likely as me being beamed up to central casting for a shot at two pages of a Woody Allen movie … yeah right. Just as I had suspected, my hands were quite unqualified for the job. They will as a result remain my old, beat-up hands that have done a lot harder work than modeling.

Rants That Really Matter

1. Professional athletes make too much money.

2. Why are the rich so rich? If 96% of us are making less than $250,000, are we just sucking up to the 4% we wish we could be?

3. If nature is God's creation, why do we treat it like a distant relative?

4. Cars choke the air, oil is fouling the water, and you say global warming is a fraud? Have you walked or ridden a bike lately?

5. WAR, what is it good for? We are always at war, how would we know peace?

6. Bureaucrats are like flies, hovering and laying slow hatching eggs in the organic democratic process.

7. Spoiled, whiney, hopelessly entitled, a-historical Americans are tourists in their own country.

8. Capitalism is a scam. It's a pyramid scheme with plenty of parking. It's an inside job.

9. No universal health care? If lack of healthcare were a base-ball stat, we have been in last place for 50 years compared to our industrialized compadres.

10. What is God? Did we invent the concept or did it invent us?

Back In Berkeley

Trying to see if my spot was still there, I go through the process of walking up to that sweet curve in the pavement as it crumbles under the roots of the mighty redwoods. This is my first day back to Berkeley after the death of my father. Berkeley, California … not to be taken lightly, as it is the last stop on the horizon. Looking out over another day as the sun burns down through the March sky. One really knows you are home when you have to dodge a ravenous seagull six miles inland.

My first day at Cal was filled with nervous wonder. Would the kids remember me, and hang with my way of looking at the world? Long story short, they did. What bliss to stand on my spot once again. To have my voice sail along Strawberry Creek through the trees and lift over the fog. Maybe I was just getting the "oddly dressed old guy yelling on the Plaza" bump. It worked for me, and before long I was snuggling into a large glove called Free Speech that fit me just fine. Let's get ready to rumble.

My Spot

There is nothing like being on my spot in Berkeley – the home of the Free Speech Movement. To a street performer or a stubum, it's all about Location Location Location. Carlos Castaneda spent a whole book trying to find the right spot to place his protagonist. An imagined but very real dot in the universe is the only reason you even showed up that day! Here I am on what we have named "Ohlone Plaza," after the original Native American residents. I'm sure the Ohlone could never have imagined Frat Boys belching to the stars, drunk on the spoils of being *so darn special.*

After a long absence from my SPOT to care for my now-deceased father, I was performing to a crowd of well-wishers. The sun, which was just peeking through two redwoods, poked me in the eye. It reminded me just how lucky I am, and how lucky this country is, to have a place like Berkeley. Just beyond the fringe of my crowd, a long time ago, Mario Savio was laughing at my lame jokes and wondering just WHAT THE HELL I was talking about. He had a great SPOT himself, and as a result, the FIRST AMENDMENT and Berkeley will forever be a tattoo on the body politic of United States History. If you deny this fact, you are sorely deprived of your duly-deserved US History.

Stoney on his spot, The Cup, UCB

BLOGS THE DAILY CALIFORNIAN
Sunday, October 20, 2013

CULTURE SHOT

Your daily dose of arts and entertainment

WEDNESDAY, OCTOBER 26, 2011

Street performance considered: Stoney Burke

TIM BERGERON/COURTESY

BY KANWALROOP SINGH | STAFF   LAST UPDATED OCTOBER 26, 2011

Yesterday, around 3 pm, in front of Dwinelle Hall, there stood the infamous Stoney Burke, in his green hair, his clown pants, and his whistle-blowing glory – cowering before a cop. The cop leaned against his bike with all the pomposity of a man on a power trip. The most atrocious thing about it was not the way he pestered Burke for allegedly being too loud – but the simple fact that he was standing in Burke's spot. He had uprooted an artist. He had disturbed a performance.

As the altercation ensued, Burke said, "This is my act. I am a comic. I have been doing this for 35 years. You know how there are reviews in the paper, well this is my review." Burke is right. He is a comedian, a performer, an artist – and an intelligent, witty one at that. The first time that I heard him last year, he denounced the tea party leader as being, "One of Hitler's testicles that got away." So not only did this police officer rob Burke of his free speech, he robbed him of his pulpit, he robbed him of his trade.

Burke repeatedly told the officer that he had nothing against him, in fact, he loved him, and that that feeling was probably strengthened ever so slightly because he had a gun. As the police officer pulled out his phone and began to talk into it, Burke joked that he was calling a helicopter and a backup team to come assassinate him. The crowd grew. People formed a large circle around Burke and the cop, almost as if to say, that they would be there, watching and listening, if anything truly criminal were to happen.

In the face of threat, Burke was a true artist. He hardly flinched. If anything, he took his cue from the crowd of students and only heightened his performance. At one point, he joked that this was all part of the act, that he had actually called the cop over for dramatic purposes. He spewed his verbal bullets at the cop, telling him he should be the one ashamed of himself. He had caused the real disturbance.

When the cop finally left, Burke said, "I am like a wart on this campus. I am only here because students before you fought for my right to stand here and tell the worst jokes known to man." It didn't take long for the self-deprecating humor to settle back in. Burke also made his most profound, pithy statement of the day, "Fuck the cops."

Justice was served.

I Am Not A Stand-Up Comic!

Even though I indeed do stand up and exercise my, dare I say, considerable skills to elicit laughter, I do not consider myself part and parcel of the "business" of comedy. You can place your two-drink minimum, cover charge, and parking fee on your plastic before this chapter even starts if you're looking for a tamed creature who aspires to sit with Jimmy on late night. Just like the tigers they have to keep in cages, lest they be unleashed on the public, I have always had a feral instinct to be outside, in the open air, where only the lumpen scrabble, cops, and God can judge me.

At one time I made the effort to trim my verbal sails and play nice with an audience more interested in the small minds on TV than the larger picture called reality. It just wasn't for me. Granted, it was and is my financial downfall. They don't call it show "business" for nothing. If you are not prepared to be canned and sold like so many oily sardines, then the spirit wounding will be permanent. I am ever so blessed to have had a place like Berkeley where the minds run wild, dreamers pontificate, and the swift political weather blows harder than a Pacific nor'easter. In my line of work, the threat of arrest and mental dismemberment is present every time I step onstage. Granted there are some excellent, highly relevant, and very funny stand-up comics who have mastered the art of humor as they tip toe through the mass culture tulips. They appear mostly to be ever so careful not to embarrass or truth tell to the master and his corporate lawyer dogs.

Not Just Every Day

Every day is just not just every day in my field of work. For every day I have stood out on the Plaza to pontificate, there is a sub event or lesson to be learned, perhaps about myself, or a simple truth revealed. Today during my second show at Cal, a tour group from China came by with 30 young people of college or high school age and happened upon my speech. I was clowning around and getting my laughs, and the tour guide came forward to explain just who they were and why they were in Berkeley. Several of his students came forward to introduce themselves, get a picture taken, have a laugh. The tour guide is chuckling as I introduce myself as the Chancellor of UCB. I pluck the plastic guitar from my bag and sing a sweetly twisted tune of Berkeley.

The tour guide is now off to the side with his large youth group. He dutifully seems to translate all my lyrics, even waving his arms like I do. Suddenly, I declare as if it were thusly proclaimed to be true, "I believe that we should have free speech like this in Tiananmen Square in China!" All of the sudden the tour guide stops translating, his arms drop to his side, and he shakes his head "NO." He will go no farther down that road with me. The kids from China are looking at me like I must have made some odd phonetic fumble that the tour guide could not handle. No, it was just freedom creeping in, it's words striking fear in the hearts of all functionaries of the State.

Bumperstickerism

Live simply, so others can simply live.

"We need the earth, the earth does not need us." – *Chief Seattle*

"You think that what you are doing is insignificant, but it must be done." – *Gandhi*

Arizona ... it's a dry hate.

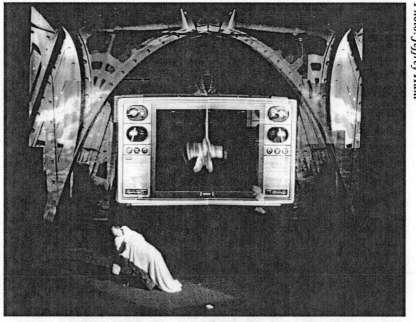

Photo: Jeffrey Hunt

Stoney in GCPW's Rare Area

Glenn Beck Turns Black

"**S**omething is happening today that is beyond the imagination," slurped Glenn Beck as he raised his eyes to the sky.

For one glorious moment Glenn Beck thought he was Black. It was he – Glenn – who helped John Brown reload his rifles at Harpers Ferry. It was the Beckmeister who, in the dead of night, helped Harriet Tubman spirit slaves out of the deepest South. As Glenn came back to earth, and gazed upon the sea of white people, he realized he had pulled off a tried-and-true scam of the oh-so-glorious right in America.

To claim that he – Glenn – worth a cool 35 million, was being shunned and put upon by American Socialism.

"Woe are we," he whined to a Jesus that was busy elsewhere, helping clean up BP oil that still coated everything but the teflonated corporate suits. Glenn had a dream last week, that he thought of last year. Dr. King had a dream that came to fruition 400 years after a nation decided to wake up. The atavistic GOP can pretend that the USA was part of the Disney channel until the Vietnam war, but most of us know the world is not a simple place, but a buffet table, slopping over with nuance and contradiction. Please keep the libraries open so that more lil' Glenn Becks are aborted in a way . . . beyond imagination. Returning Glenn's mansion in Connecticut to the Native Americans would be a good first step in "restoring honor."

Fakebook

Having just seen the film "Social Network," one can't walk out into the sunlight and not be grateful that reality is still very much what we walk through, and that sitting in front of a flat, dimly lit screen is just another moment not interacting in the real world. The amount of privacy that has been chipped away in the last 20 years is like the glaciers in the arctic that continue to melt, in part due to the tsunami of machines all requiring vast amounts of energy. I've often wondered, if the world were a person, would it be our "friend?" George Orwell would be shocked that we volunteer for big brothers eternal gaze. We pass on private information like it was a glass of water at Club Med.

The beasts and bullies that have yellow streaks tattooed on their backs enjoy the cyber power of anonymity. It is quite possible we are only seeing the beginning of total robot culture that will eventually diminish the very things that make us human. Some scenes in the film do have a ring of truth to them. How words hurt, how money perverts even the young and naive. I'm sure it sounds like I'd be the person who thought only birds should fly, or that cameras stole the soul of those captured a century ago.

Even in a cyber hurricane it's not only possible, but necessary to take "shelter from the storm." Already people in the USA sit and watch almost eight hours of TV a day. Merge a cyber life into that, and it's no wonder fewer people VOTE in this country than in Iraq! Eventually no one will have any real friends. Just a shadow of ether and words that are posted to a page. No one ever talks about how lonely we have become, or lacking in physical contact, as if all these postings lead to a bliss-filled social life. My father, who passed away last year at age 86, never wrote an email in his life, and the day after he passed there were no results of his life recorded in a Google search. Yet he lived a rich, full life with hundreds of "real" friends.

What is my point here? That even if you turned off all the machines in your computer life, the fiber and depth of your humanness would still reflect on all of those around you. In the book *Nineteen Eighty-Four* Winston had just a small space in his room where BIG BROTHER could not see. Where is our window of privacy? Has it been left open to the cold breeze of apathy?

Whenever I look at my "Fakebook" page now, I regret answering anything at all. Millions of years from now, people will wonder why the word and meaning of FRIEND was hijacked. The movie "Social Network" is the glorification of the Nazi nerds and their insatiable cult of wealth. No one can eat or live in cyberspace, but a little bit of our soul dies everytime we walk by a homeless human struggling, or a senior who suffers alone in a rest home. Humans, not Robots, will in the end inherit the earth.

I Was There!

Have you ever played this mind game? The older you get the more fun it is to play, but this game can be engaged in for no good reason at all, This is where you turn your hat sideways and present your best Forest Gump smile as you rattle off the close calls and breathtaking lifetime dramas. Yes, this is that chapter.

9/11

I had this idea at one time that I was going to parlay my layoff from a tech-related job in SF, and move to NYC to be a "real" actor. I had loaded up my life and packed into a Greyhound that departed Detroit in late August 2001. I checked into a cheap hotel down on the Bowery and began collating my resumé for mailing to all the important casting agencies.

On the fourth day of my arrival I was walking near Washington Square park near 10th Avenue when I heard the distinct roar of jet engines. I looked up in time to see the gray underbelly of the jet as it flew low oh so low over the tall buildings. As I headed down the street I turned the corner and looked up to see the top of the World Trade Center with a large black gash at the top. It was as if some Zorro from the underworld had left his mark. The stack of unmailed headshots didn't seem that important anymore. Onlookers gathered to stare in horror. None of us knew or even could imagine what had just happened. Like a giant barbecue grill gone mad, it smoldered, spit wretched plumes of smoke, and burned and burned. Just when we thought we had seen it all, another explosion and fire can be seen farther down the WTC's facade. I still think this must be a tragic accident of some sort. Then a tourist in the crowd is showing us his camcorder which shows a plane circling around and plunging into the WTC from the opposite side of our viewing angle. From that moment on we knew it was no twist of fate, or accident. It was what it was, and I saw it with my own eyes. When I watched the first building crumble like a sand castle, and shrieks of grief rose from the crowd, it was time for me to go back to the hotel, pull the covers over my head and wonder what the hell I had just seen.

This is the point in the story where I could score a lot of points by oozing a sugary conspiracy down your throat, or just plain make up stuff I know nothing about. I know what I saw, and I felt emotionally crushed about it most of the time. One day, I was packed, on the elevator down, and ready to leave NYC. The hotel desk clerk called me aside. It was a message from the temp agency saying I had a job! It was at the top of the MetLife Time Building in the mailroom. Considering the anthrax killer was powdering envelopes all over Manhattan, I figured a spot had opened up and I was next in line in some strange twist of fate. Round and round I'd go with my little cart at the top of the MetLife Building, delivering mail and looking south over the city at the WTC still burning even three months after the attack.

The Earthquake of 1989, San Francisco

The time was 5 o'clock in the afternoon. I was an SF state student working on three term papers and listening to the SF Giants playing cross-bay rivals The Oakland A's in the World Series.

The LA Riots, the Rodney King Verdict

I can remember talking to a large crowd at UCLA going off about police brutality and the fang-like mentality of LAPD. I had seen on TV a million times the electric wires dangling from Rodney King's body as he stumbled to his feet only to be beaten down by clubs and feet. Tonight I learn that Rodney King has passed away. Fate chose his to expose the biggest gang in CA. That would be the LAPD.

"The only way to survive history is to enter the Mythfire."
– Arnie Passman

Stoney, Arnie Passman, Wavy Gravy at
Peace Symbol Celebration party

STONEY DAY!

November 14, 2006
Stoney, A Clown Who Rabble Rouses
In Defense Of Free Speech, Day.

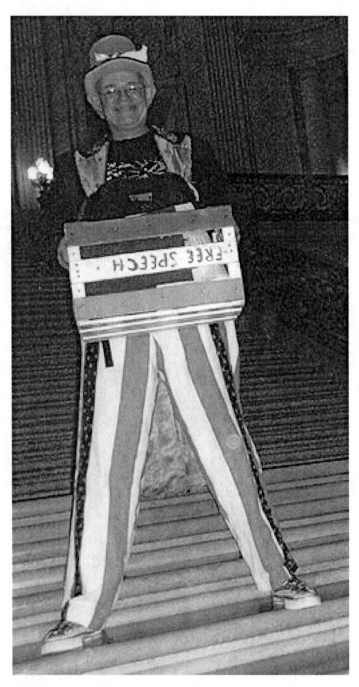

Free Speech Box at San Francisco City Hall, Stoney Day

Proclamation
City and County of San Francisco

Whereas, The world needs clowns like Stoney Burke; and,

Whereas, Stoney has delivered wit and laugh since he was a young boy; and,

Whereas, He even strategically flunked out of catholic school in fourth grade; and,

Whereas, He has stood on a plaza or in a free speech area, reading newspapers and commenting on current events for the last 30 years; and,

Whereas, He has been arrested so many times for expressing his views and dressing up as, of course, a clown, Uncle Sam, and many others; now, therefore, be it,

Resolved, That the Board of Supervisors of the City and County of San Francisco designates November 14, 2006, as the official Stoney, A Clown Who Rabble Rouses In Defense of Free Speech, Day; and be it,

Further Resolved, That the Board of Supervisors of the City and County of San Francisco listens to Stoney Burke's plan for world peace utilizing One Million Soapboxes, the day Stoney receives his proclamation.

This resolution was passed by the Board of Supervisors of the City and County of San Francisco on November 14, 2006.

Proclamation for Stoney Day

Public Access Icon

SwarzaNickel

SF Supervisor Sandoval and Stoney, Stoney Day

STONEY BURKE'S GREATEST HITS
1977-2007

THE '80s

#1. OPENING SHORT, MUSIC: ESKIMO, 2 mins, Dir: Lauren Hatvany

#2. STONEY AT UC BERKELEY, 1985, 6 mins

#3. THE POPE COMES TO SAN FRANCISCO, 1987, 6 mins, Dir: Lauren Hatvany

#4 AN AMERICAN IN AMERICA (excerpt), 1980, 31 mins, Dir: Kage Jonsson, Swedish TV

#5 CITIZEN (excerpt), 1982, 2 mins, Dir: George Coates/William Farley

#6 STONEY DOES DALLAS, 1984, 15 mins, Dir: Bob Hercules

THE '90s

#7 OPENING SHORT: ANDRE FENLEY, Downstairs Productions

#8 STONEY AT HIS ALMA MATER, SAN FRANCISCO STATE UNIVERSITY, 1991, 6.0 mins

#9 STONEY DOES HOUSTON, 1992, 15 mins, Dir: Bob Hercules

#10 NEWT DRIVES A CHRYSLER, 1994, 15 mins, JT Productions, Ann Arbor Public Access

THE 2000s

#11 OPENING SHORT: ANDRE FENLEY, Downstairs Productions

#12 RECALL ARNOLD, 2003, 6 mins, Berkeley Community Media

#13 BARTLEBY (excerpt), 2000, 3 mins, Dir: Jonathon Parker

#14 MATRIX RELOADED (excerpt), 2003, 2.0 mins, Dir: Wachowski Bros

#15 STONEY DOES MANHATTAN, 2004, 15 mins, Editor: Moby Theobold

All of these selections, and many more, can be viewed
on Stoney's YouTube channel.

Stoney's YouTube Of Fame

Channel: STONEYSPEAKS

1. Matrix Reloaded
2. John McTaint
3. An American in America
4. Mock City Council
5. Citizen
6. Bartleby
7. RareArea
8. Mock Up on Mu
9. Stoney Does Houston
10. 25 years of STONEY SPEAKS

The Real Wayne and Garth: Public Access TV's Eccentric Survivors

by Adam Grossberg

As the clock inches toward 7 p.m., the middle-aged operators start their countdown behind a pane of glass. "Bring it up, okay, go to studio," commands Steve, the long-bearded director. There's a pause. A black screen flickers. "I am – it's not going!" insists an equally long-bearded man named Marcel sitting to his right, pressing one button after another. At last, the image of Moby Theobald, the made-up pirate, flashes onto the screen, and Steve and Marcel exhale deeply.

"Welcome one and all to episode 128 of 'Watch This!'" Theobald says, bounding onto the stage. The lone audience member, sitting at the back of the classroom-turned-studio, claps his approval.

This is public access television, beamed into thousands of homes across Berkeley and the East Bay. "Watch This!" an hour-long variety show, is one of dozens of programs airing on Berkeley's Community Media, a public access stalwart and one of the last of a dying breed. On any given night, Channel 28 (BeTV for short) plays host to a range of local programming – from the politically charged talk show "Stoney Speaks" to "Frank Moore's Unlimited Possibilities," which features a naked, quadriplegic host and a series of equally naked guests engaged in what can only be described as softcore porn. A typical '80s "Wayne's World" aesthetic generally prevails.

"You're always picturing some guy dressed in a wizard costume with a blue screen in the background," Jeff Kimmich, BeTV access facilitator, says. "We put on what you give us. That's kind of the best and the worst part of the place."

The idea of public access television is simple: government-funded non-profit TV stations like BeTV typically provide training, equipment, and studio space for citizens to produce their own television shows. The shows are then broadcast on a channel designated solely for local programming. The principles behind these stations emerged during the infancy of cable TV in the early 1970s, when media advocates argued that local communities should have access to this powerful communication tool.

Today, the Internet has replaced most of the functions of public access television – community engagement, self-expression, voyeurism – and cash-strapped cities throughout the country have slashed funding to community stations. But in Berkeley, this antiquated relic is still hanging on: Berkeley Community Media remains a bubbling community of creative eccentrics eager to "be TV."

"Stoney Speaks"

In the smaller of two studios at Berkeley Community Media's office – a series of converted classrooms on the vast Berkeley High School campus – longtime public access producer Stoney Burke finishes taping the most recent episode of his show, "Stoney Speaks." Burke has been producing the show since 1985, years before BeTV went on the air. (A short-lived community studio was open in the mid-'70s, but a series of disputes between the city and the cable companies kept local programming largely off the air until the launch of BeTV in 1994.)

Burke uses his monthly time slot to rant about local and national politics, and to give voice to local Bay Area characters. "I like putting people on TV that have never been on TV," Burke says, sitting next to tonight's guest, "Bishop Joey," of the First

Church of the Last Laugh, a satirical, faux-religious group.

Burke, 59, has a strip of dyed green hair ringing his otherwise bald head. Tonight, he's wearing a tattered burlap sack that covers his whole body. Next to him, Bishop Joey wears an ersatz clergyman's cloak and a fez and wields a 12-inch plastic bone like a wand. They sit in front of a set decorated with political posters, slogans, and drawings. They call themselves "broke-butt clowns" and do a sort of Laurel and Hardy give and take. "When people have the remote in their hand and they're switching channels, they stop, and go, 'What the hek was that?'" Burke says. "That doesn't look like anything you've ever seen on a blog or something like that."

Before there was quality streaming video, says BeTV programming coordinator Arielle Elizabeth, public access was the most viable option for distributing and watching independent content. "People watched TV to see what their community was doing. Now, things have changed." These days, Elizabeth says, people "go looking to YouTube to learn things, and to hear different ideas and thoughts. They don't flip through TV."

For Burke, though, the allure of television remains strong. He's a Berkeley legend who has been performing his political clown act on UC Berkeley's Sproul Plaza since the late '70s. His television show is an extension of his street performance, a way to reach a larger audience. "This is cheaper for me to do than buy a bunch of giant computers . . . work at a keyboard or some stupid thing. That's not TV," he says. "Here they give you a technician. All you have to do is do your thing and fill your space, and it goes right on the air, reaches about 20,000 people."

Twenty thousand is a stretch. BeTV's Channel 28 – along with Channel 135, which is reserved for government programming – reaches about 17,000 homes throughout Berkeley and parts of neighboring Albany, Emeryville, and North Oakland, as part of Comcast and AT&T cable packages. But, clearly, not every cable subscriber watches BeTV. It is impossible to track the exact

viewership because BeTV isn't included in any Nielsen rating programs. 'They say with cable access, take it down to about 1,000
[viewers per show]," Burke acknowledges. By comparison, Burke
uploaded about 20 videos to YouTube last year and has had a total
of 2,700 views. Sixteen people subscribe to his channel.

The exposure public access provides is vital for Burke, but
he holds out hope for greater notoriety. "I'm still looking for my
William Hung moment," he says, referring to the American Idol
star turn, "that one moment in media history where they go, 'Did
you see what that guy did? It was the funniest thing.' I'm still looking for that moment."

"Watch This!"

On one 1999 episode of "StoneySpeaks," Burke interviewed
a local comic book artist who had never been on television. On
March 24 of this year, that guest, Moby Theobald, aired his 128th
show on Be TV. "I was just blown away by the whole idea," Theobald
recalls. "A person can put on their own show. This is amazing!"

Shortly after appearing on "StoneySpeaks," Theobald decided
to produce a variety show like the ones he grew up watching. In
May 2001, he filmed his first episode of "Watch This!" Eleven years
later, the show's format is remarkably similar – a mix of come-
dic monologue and pre-filmed sketches, which Theobald writes,
shoots, edits, and acts in, playing most of the roles in various cos-
tumes and disguises. His make-up kit includes about 20 different
mustaches.

Theobald, who produces a show every two or three weeks, sees
it as "a way of being validated, a way of saying, 'Oh, you have meaning.'" He just wishes he could get paid for it. "I guess the dream
would be somebody saying, 'Hey kid, I'm gonna make you a star!
Come over here, sign this, sign this,'" Theobald says in his gruffest
agent voice, pantomiming a cigar in hand. "A bunch of cast members on Saturday Night Live got discovered through Internet sites.

But that's not a plan, that's like saying, 'My retirement plan is I'm going to win the lottery.' Yeah, work on that luck, buddy."

Stoney Burke "pumping up the '90s."

The Axis Of Public Access

I feel sorry for any community whose population is paying cable or satellite TV bills, and have no Public Access TV station. Or worse yet where they have a fake one. A high-paid media manager type who collects paychecks for putting tapes in a machine. They are being are being deprived of the fundamental right to speak, inform, and produce local TV with no commercial intent. A public access TV station is the people's antidote to the concentration of corporate media power that sucks the life out of our brains on an average of eight hours a day. It is a place where people can make TV, instead of being a victim of it. Noted author Scoop Nisker, on his long-ago SF radio show, used to end every broadcast by saying, "If you don't like the news, go out and make some of your own."

My personal definition of what a public access station is, was my ability to produce and broadcast "StoneySpeaks." Under that moniker, I squeeze the famous, and never-will-be famous, into my version of late night TV. From the smartest adult film actress of all time, Nina Hartley, to the abrasively off-key crooning of street singer, Rick Starr. They all have made "StoneySpeaks TV" one the most exciting non-commercial ventures I've ever had the pleasure to be a part of. Back in the mid 1980s a UC Berkeley student Lauren Hatvany, said, "Hey, let's go to CH25 in San Francisco, Public Access and make TV!" She was, and is, a talented producer, as well as a good friend. She produced "The Pope Comes to San Francisco" and many, many other episodes of "StoneySpeaks TV," most of which can be seen on YouTube. The only public access station to ever to outright remove, censor, and hold fast to a life-long ban of "Stoney Speaks" was sadly, in my hometown of Romeo, Michigan.

My first and only episode was a taped panel discussion in San Francisco of performance artist Karen Finley. As I watched at home on premier night, the screen suddenly went black about halfway through the 30-minute episode. Next the phone rings, it's the station manager Jack Applecore. He's explaining to me that he just got off the phone with the local Republican Supervisor Gary Shooktree, who was so outraged at the content that he demanded it be removed from the broadcast immediately! I must have touched a nerve the size of a yam. Fifteen years previously his father, James ShookTree, the Justice of the Peace, had run IGGY POP out of town after a bawdy but legendary STOOGES show at the "Mothers" music venue in Romeo. I was there that night, when the music died, and the venue was closed forever. Son, like father, right down to the APPLECORE, was doing a GOP body slam to local culture as I knew it. It was too late, I had seen the crazed, determined snarl on Iggy Pop's face before he fled the Mothers half naked, and hid in an alley nearby until the police took him into custody. Iggy went off to Berlin to record with David Bowie. I stayed in Romeo. That was rock 'n' roll.

If there are two words that scare the hek out of Republicans, it's PUBLIC and ACCESS. Instead of putting my parents at risk of another bullet hole in the mailbox, or worse, I put my Weapon: Mouth back in the holster. I incorrectly assumed this glitch in small-town Free Speech would be corrected in due time. It was not to be. With the blessings of the local Republican leadership, Jack Applecore ran the station for the next 20 years as if he owned it. "StoneySpeaks" was quickly removed. End of discussion. Taped episodes of "The Rising Tide" with GOP host Haley Barbour quickly filled my series slot. Most public access stations have a written agreement with local government to ensure that the public had "access." The key word is "most." Jack Applecore forbade forever independent producers. With a loyal GOP base covering his tail, he made darn sure that Iron Gate of media freedom was locked and secure. Many years later Jack forced to close the already paid for building that housed the media center. As soon as the lock clicked on the door, Jack was running unopposed for the same GOP township supervisor seat that the ShookTree boys had held 20 years ago.

To this day, the building sits empty, abandoned, and forgotten. My late father asked me one time why he had to go to San Francisco to be on my TV show, "Don't "we" have a public access station?" What do you mean "we" I replied to my father. Sadly, father and son in the village we both loved, were never provided the opportunity to walk up the street together for a TV show. I thank Kage Jonsson for putting both my mother and father in the film "An American in America" when we filmed in Romeo. Because film is forever!

Stoney, Penelope Houston, and Jello Biafra on "StoneySpeaks TV"

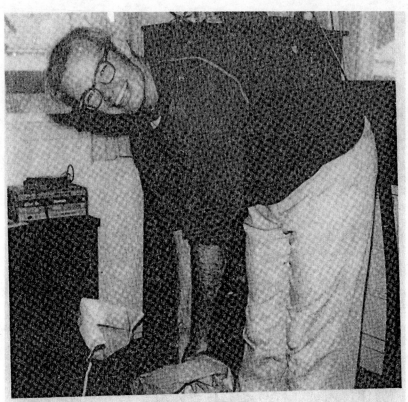

STONEY BURKE

Stoney Burke comes to WBRW

Stoney Burke, a Romeo native, brings his unique brand of satire to WBRW this week.

"Stoney Speaks" is the name of Burke's talk show, which currently airs in San Francisco.

Burke started his performing career as a street mime at the University of California, Berkley campus. He appeared in the movie, "Citizen" with Whoopie Goldberg and was recently a member of the George Coats Performance Works original production of "Rare Area."

Burke was also the subject of a documentary made by a film crew from Sweden. The documentary, which has been shown all over the world, features many scenes shot in Romeo.

"Stoney Speaks" comes to WBRW . . . Once!

FRANK MOORE / Chicago Art Institute. In October of 2013, the world lost a true genius, and free speech hero – Frank Moore. Public access TV was never the same once he was allowed to bring his love tent, "eroplay," and poetry to the small screen. RIP Frank, you will be missed. I've had my tough days, and Frank was always there to point the way.

The Queen of Anti-fashion Dee Dee Russell, Public Access Icon, San Francisco, CA.

Ann Arbor Public Access Icon SAFETY GIRL. Her safe sex talk show was so audacious when it premiered that one viewer called 911 to complain. That's FREE SPEECH!

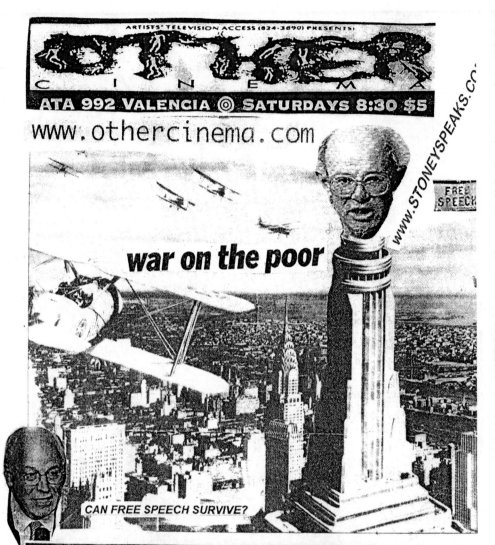

ARTISTS' TELEVISION ACCESS (824-3890) PRESENTS:

OTHER CINEMA

ATA 992 VALENCIA ◎ SATURDAYS 8:30 $5

www.othercinema.com

war on the poor

FREE SPEECH

...WWW.STONEYSPEAKS.CO...

CAN FREE SPEECH SURVIVE?

SAT. 3/18: *THE UNAUTHORIZED BIOGRAPHY OF DICK CHENEY* +

On the third anniversary of the **U.S.** invasion of **Iraq**, we invite all dissenters to vent some righteous outrage at arguably the war's prime mover, **(Vice) President Cheney**. We were lucky enough to snag this **Canadian** made-for-TV expose that shines the light of day on this sleazy, greasy war pig, a man who extols the virtues of torture, and wants land-mine production brought back online. So let's call it a **Pig Roast**, with pork (and tofu) sausages freely dispensed. **Stoney Burke** will emcee and **Pod** will deejay, setting up a block of scorching agit-prop, with **Ed Holmes** in Cheney drag, the **Yes Men** on the campaign trail, **Bryan Boyce**'s ventriloquist trick, and hell yeah, a **Hummer** bonfire! Our post-protest lounge opens at 7:30, showcasing DJ Pod's latest CD releases.

LIL' HITLER FROM HALLIBURTON!

What Does It All Mean?

Every time I set foot on a stage of my choosing, I ask the same thing, "What does it all mean?" My version of wealth is measured in something other than money. Being broke, or in debt, sets your mind and spirit on a quest for truth. My currency is the smile on a face, or the sparkle of truth-dust that I choke up laughing about.

One half of the world lives on less than $2.00 a day. That's a cold, humorless fact. Well, I know I'm doing better than that. I have to go to the gym to work off my excess calories. 96% of the population in the USA makes less than $250,000 a year. The other 4% surfs in comfort. The great middle class has been melted away like a polar bear's dinner plate. "Socialism for the rich, Capitalism for the rest of you," is a lyric I remember from a band called MDC.

The Three Js Of Free Speech

To make it in this racket, you must be prepared to face the three Js:

1. Jeered
2. Jumped
3. Jailed

These ongoing threats will hunt you down and get you unless you unleash a hurricane of guffaws over your left shoulder. Jeering is the grey area between disagreement and going for a nearby tree branch. Jumped is not making enough "friends" of your cause to allow you to walk safely off campus or city property. Jailing is the system's way of using an axe to remove a fly from its nose.

Not long ago, the UPCD parked a bicycle cop on my spot, no doubt his message was that I should not OCCUPY that space any longer. On his approach, I quickly put a lot of distance and a garbage can between us. I slipped around to the other side of a cement tree planter – about the distance where his pepper spray wouldn't reach me. Is this a pre-arrest warning? Or have I already been arrested, and is UC Berkeley just a holding pen for those of us who are still silly enough to think we are free?

The Last Laugh

A few years ago, Leonard Pitt and I received a call from one Bishop Joey. "I need three rope-robed, sandal-stepping Monks to cook up a ritual for a church member." In no time at all, the three of us met and agreed to scour our vast knowledge of HA. Bishop Joey agreed to reveal its true purpose later.

So it was one hop to the left, a Three Stooge's triple bypass, double take, which blurred into a skittered, sideways soft-sandal tap to the right. Having done that, we stood at attention to deliver a well murmured discourse containing no less than six vowels that collided like a shopping cart hitting a stack of water balloons at high speed.

Finally I asked, "Who is this for?" The Bishop took his hand out of the till, and looked up at the clock. "It's for Ken Kesey. It's his last laugh."

As Kesey's Beyond Further party was drawing to a close, we stopped by to shake his hand. His radiant smile seemed to melt whatever fog had lingered in this life. Ever since then, I've had the feeling that all of us, just like in his novel *Cuckoos Nest*, would somehow clear the barbed-wire fence right behind Chief Bromden.

Dick Gregory and Will Durst
To see two of the best political comics in the USA, on the same stage,
representing almost 50 years of satire, was a night to remember.

Bishop Joey and Stoney Burke
On April 1st, every year for the last 35 years in San Francisco, the big
bass drum of Bishop Joey leads a thousand-clown march through the
streets. Here is St. Stupid himself on "StoneySpeaks TV," Berkeley
Community Media.

"America! ... Put The Guns Down, And Come Out With Your Heart Open!"

♔

When the floundering fathers of our flawed Constitution wrote the Second Amendment, the only existing guns at the time took five minutes to load and shoot one steel ball in the general direction of its intended target. "A well regulated militia," was not referring to the ten-items-or-less register at Walmart. When you check out a book from the library, it's assumed you can read. When you apply for a driver's license, you have to know how to drive. But to get an automatic weapon in America, you merely have to exist. There is a bizarre disconnect in the gun-and-run crowd where answers to very complex social problems are simplified with sick blog posts or the pull of a trigger. It's an ideology rooted in hopelessness, despair, and self destruction. No bullet can care for a child, or bring laughter to a heart. It really does take the free will of a freedom-loving people not to coddle the bottom-feeders among us. As the O'Jays sang many years ago, "If you are not on that peace train, I feel sorry for you."

Epilogue

One of, if not my favorite film about buskers is an old black-and-white classic titled "Sidewalks of London" (1938). It tells the tale of street monologist Charles Saggers (Charles Laughton) who adds talented dancer and pickpocket Libby (Vivien Leigh) to his sidewalk act in the London theater district. Dapper theater patron Harry Prentiss (Rex Harrison) happens by, sees Libby dance, and is impressed. At first Charles becomes jealous and enraged at her new-found success inside the theater. Charles tells her in so many words how ungrateful she is, and predictably loses her love forever. Eventually Libby falls in love with Harry and goes on to stardom, leaving the street life and Charles far behind. For many years Charles continues busking in front of the theater, as he always has, while Libby goes on to live a life he could only dream of.

Many years later, by chance, they run into each other at the same theater where they started so many years ago. She wistfully recounts with him their humble beginnings together. Libby is overcome with guilt, and wants very badly to share her type of success with him. She sets up an audition for him with her reluctant producers. They agree to give him a chance, just as a favor to her. The audition proves difficult. Charles passionately struggles to convey his worn-out street shtick to a handful of cynical and unenthused casting agents who roll their eyes at every inflection in Charles performance. The large empty theater seems to swallow him whole. He fails miserably at the audition. Afterwards Charles surrenders to defeat, sees the light, and conveys his bitterness to a tearful Libby. He leaves the theater by the back door, and is back on the street from whence he came. In the line that defines the whole movie, he turns back to the theater one last time and says:

"You'll never get me inside. I've been outside too long."

This book is dedicated to those that have been outside too long, tried too hard to pass the audition, or may have failed at life's fortune. But despite it all, in their own way, have found a spot to call their own. Charlie Chaplin perhaps said it better than I ever could. "Life is a tragedy when seen in close-up, but a comedy in long shot."

As the O'Jays sang so long ago,
"If you are not on that peace train, I feel sorry for you."

Glossary

BIKO PLAZA ... Sproul Plaza renamed in honor of Stephen Biko of South Africa during the anti-apartheid demos in and around the San Francisco Bay Area.

DIAG ... At the University of Michigan in Ann Arbor, the Diag is a large open space in the middle of the university's Central Campus. Originally known as the Diagonal Green, the Diag derives its name from the many sidewalks running near or through it in diagonal directions. It is one of the busiest sites on the university campus, hosting a variety of events including outdoor concerts, fundraisers, demonstrations, and sun bathing. (Wikipedia)

HA ... Ha ha, humor, satire, etc.

HOLLYWOOD ... A place you should never go, unless they call your name. Listen to a conch shell and you hear the ocean, listen to the sounds in the woods, and you hear the birds. Listen to an empty Coca Cola can being swept across an empty parking lot ... that's the sound of Hollywood.

IWT ... I Was There ... not merely a recounting of some overpriced moment that could be had for a price, but a tick of the clock of fate that had my name on it, in person.

OC ... Original Crazy. Those who have have managed to be crazy in and around any metropolitan area or college campus for a period of 20 years or more.

Ohlone Plaza ... Renamed from Dwinelle Plaza for the original Native inhabitants of the place upon whose land I speak upon. I feel the thunder under my feet, and the seagulls disperse when Mother Earth's blessings are clearly spoken from this area. All free speech areas are at heart and in spirit belonging to the Native people who were silenced and relocated so that the concept of "free" speech could thrive.

Robot Culture ... A world where every-day decisions are ruled by electronic devices, with a human chaperone who repeats "I don't know."

Scam ... Any event or program that I can't understand taking place while people sit idly by wondering why it does.

SFSU ... San Francisco State University, San Francisco, California, the Alma Mater of Stoney Burke class of 1991, and Johnny Mathis.

Stubum ... Student, bum, infomaniac, believer in the cause. If a bit of knowledge can be slightly engaging in a quiet moment, it can be raged into the insightful rant of the day. A stubum picks the brain of the brilliant with the only tuition paid – a cup of coffee at the Med.

Suit ... Usually grey, spun from polyester, and containing heavily armed Government agent who is friendly, but drenched in ill intent.

The Beast on the Hill ... University of California at Berkeley for instance, or any other evil entity that throws its weight around, and bellows for more and more power. It could be Pole Town in Detroit, fighting off General Motors, or the liberal Nuns staring down the Pope in the Vatican. Even in your small town or village there is a Beast on the Hill. Get a running start, it's king of the hill all over again.

THE F WORD ... Any word beginning with F that may result in jail or a tasering if uttered in the company of your class enemy.

TOWNIE ... Here today, here tomorrow. I don't just pretend to live here, I do. The toughest part of speaking at college campus is that every four years, you have to say good bye and say hello to those who stood in the rain or had a laugh before the drudge of a Chem lab. Your best friends are those that stand like trees, year after year, weathering the fast-food college curriculum, to put knowledge and leisure on slow cook.

UCB ... University of California at Berkeley.